I0189496

WHEN GOD
SEEMS DISTANT

WHEN GOD SEEMS DISTANT

SURPRISING WAYS GOD
DEEPENS OUR FAITH
AND DRAWS US NEAR

KYLE STROBEL
AND JOHN COE

BakerBooks

a division of Baker Publishing Group
Grand Rapids, Michigan

© 2026 by Kyle Strobel and John Coe

Published by Baker Books
a division of Baker Publishing Group
Grand Rapids, Michigan
BakerBooks.com

Printed in the United States of America

All rights reserved. No part of this publication may be reproduced, stored in a retrieval system, or transmitted in any form or by any means—for example, electronic, photocopy, recording—without the prior written permission of the publisher. The only exception is brief quotations in printed reviews.

Library of Congress Cataloging-in-Publication Data
Names: Strobel, Kyle, 1978– author | Coe, John H. author
Title: When God seems distant : surprising ways God deepens our faith and draws us near / Kyle Strobel, John Coe.
Description: Grand Rapids, Michigan : Baker Books, a division of Baker Publishing Group, [2026]
Identifiers: LCCN 2025027321 | ISBN 9781540905321 paperback | ISBN 9781540905383 casebound | ISBN 9781493452897 ebook
Subjects: LCSH: Spiritual life—Christianity | Spiritual formation
Classification: LCC BV4501.3 .S7855 2026
LC record available at https://lccn.loc.gov/2025027321

Unless otherwise indicated, Scripture quotations are from The Holy Bible, English Standard Version® (ESV®). Copyright © 2001 by Crossway, a publishing ministry of Good News Publishers. Used by permission. All rights reserved. ESV Text Edition: 2016

Scripture quotations labeled NKJV are from the New King James Version®. Copyright © 1982 by Thomas Nelson. Used by permission. All rights reserved.

Cover design by Studio Gearbox

The authors are represented by Illuminate Literary Agency, www.illuminateliterary.com.

Baker Publishing Group publications use paper produced from sustainable forestry practices and postconsumer waste whenever possible.

26 27 28 29 30 31 32   7 6 5 4 3 2 1

To Jody and Jeanie Humber.
Thank you for your encouragement and
your desire to discover the Lord in all seasons of life.
You are in our hearts. We are grateful for you and your
openheartedness to us and to the Lord. Bless you as you
continually draw near to him to seek his face.

CONTENTS

1

Experience Beyond
Expectation

Consistently in Scripture, God's people are baffled by
how he chooses to lead.

God's shepherding confounds expectation. He delivers his
people from Egypt with visible power and miracles, only to
march them into hunger and thirst. He leads his people to
Mount Sinai to draw them near to himself and then scares
them nearly to death as he descends with fire and fury on
the mountaintop. He conquers death in resurrection, telling
his followers he will never leave them, and then he leaves,
ascending back to the Father, causing them to wonder about
his presence until they receive his Spirit.

Throughout Scripture, and from brothers and sisters
throughout history, we discover wisdom about navigating
these confusing experiences with the Lord. But we also discover that life with God is not just one sort of experience but
includes various seasons of the soul. There are seasons of

abundance, where life is full of joy, excitement, and deliverance from darkness. There are seasons of questioning why God would lead us into a desert and into spiritual hunger and thirst. There are times we grapple with the confusion of standing at a cross when we expected to be celebrating a conquering King.

John and I grew up in churches that forgot how to talk about these things. We were left to make sense of these experiences on our own. We didn't consider how to understand seasons of abundance and joy, or what is often called consolation. We just assumed this was how things were supposed to be. It was the experience of God's absence that was so confusing. When we found ourselves in the desert—dry as dust—we had no idea what the Lord was doing. So we just assumed the Lord wasn't doing *anything at all in those places*. But even more confusing than the desert were seasons where the Lord led us into experiences of his absence—what is sometimes called desolation. In these places we really felt lost; in these places we thought the Lord had abandoned us.

We didn't realize at the time that our experience was exactly what the disciples went through. None of them expected Jesus the Messiah to act like he did. He confused his disciples. None of them understood what they were signing up for by following him. Repeatedly, the bottom dropped out from their lives, and they had to wonder, *Lord, what are you doing in this?* Jesus continues to work this way in our lives today, undermining our expectations about what God is like and what he does. Jesus continues to reveal the good news and show us that our own ways are mired in falsehoods. Throughout his ministry, Jesus tore down as much as he built up, and that is exactly why following him can feel so confusing.

For some, this might sound like bad news. For many, perhaps, as with Jesus's disciples, this is not what you signed up for when you started following Jesus. This is not what you expected. None of us fully appreciate what life with the Lord will be like and where he will lead. But there is a choice we must make: Will we follow him into the dark and embrace his way of life, or will we fall into superficiality? Will we live lives shaped by his, or will we try to use him to get the life we want?

Feeling Lost and Confused

Although John and I had very different stories of salvation (I grew up in the church, and John became a Christian at the end of high school), we ended up walking through similar frustrations. After his conversion, John went to a church that focused on deep study of Scripture, and he was saturated with knowledge, devotion, and a vision of Christian faithfulness. My own experience focused more on exuberant praise, numerical growth, and serving the church. Both of us found our early years rich and rewarding. We both experienced incredible joy in the Christian life, and we both grew tremendously.

Although no one taught us this explicitly, through these early experiences of excitement, joy, and delighting in God, we began to equate our experience *with God's presence itself*. We talked about God "showing up" when we felt passionate, as if God's presence could be judged by our feelings. So when we experienced joy and excitement and the goodness of obedience, we felt like we could rest in the presence and comfort of the Lord. But years later something else emerged. We grew tired. We became bored. We kept on serving, learning, praising, and giving—in all the ways we knew how—but the initial joy wore off.

Had we done something wrong? Were we supposed to do more? Was our past sin catching up with us, revealing that God hadn't really saved us after all? Was God punishing us? Worries and struggles rose from our hearts, and we didn't know what to do.

Our churches put us on a good path when we were young in the faith, but we were given less direction as we grew, and even less in these darker seasons. It was like the confusion of puberty made its way into our Christian maturation, and no one was willing to talk about it. What we did share with others was met with well-meaning but often unhelpful responses.

Keep going.

Try harder.

Do more.

Our efforts began to feel more and more pointless. So we kept learning, serving, and growing, but our souls felt dry as dust, and we were left wondering if we misunderstood what the "rivers of living water" were. Our praise felt like our lips were moving while our hearts wandered far from him. So we kept toiling away at what used to work. John studied more. I tried to praise with more vigor. We both felt lost.

These struggles, and the questions they raise, have been the focus of our lives and work for decades. In differing ways, for the past thirty years we have both focused our lives on what growth into the likeness of Jesus is actually like. We have found immense freedom and joy in a deeper journey with the Lord in the truth. It is this journey we are inviting you to take.

This is a book about growing in the faith and learning to navigate the confusing process of transformation. God's ways are not our ways, a fact we often forget. We feel lost and assume that means *we are lost*. We feel dry, tired, and bored, and we imagine that God is withholding himself from us until we try harder and get ourselves together. Our assumptions, expectations, and beliefs need to be transformed by the Lord, who loved to say, "You've heard it said . . . But I say to you . . ." If you have heard—directly or indirectly— "Try harder" or "Just do more" or even "Try these spiritual disciplines," then we have good news for your soul. If you have gotten to a point in your faith where you feel lost or are wondering where God went or where the joy of salvation vanished to, then we hope this will encourage you. If you ever feel like you're wandering in a desert, desperate for the waters of life, you've come to the right place.

Where Scripture turns our attention, of course, is Jesus. Jesus is the place where our experiences with God are made clear. Jesus is the perfect Son of God, and yet the Spirit sent him to the wilderness to be tempted by Satan (Matt. 4:1). Jesus is the One who, in desperate prayer, asked the Father to let this cup pass from him (Matt. 26:39). Jesus is the One who cried out, "My God, my God, why have you forsaken me?" (Matt. 27:46). Jesus is the true Son who nonetheless learned obedience through suffering (Heb. 5:8). To follow Jesus is to walk through these desert places and to come to know that the Lord guides us through the desert to the promised land.

Out for a Sail: A Parable

Seeing this in the life of Jesus makes sense, but experiencing it in our own lives is often bewildering. An image might help. Imagine yourself afloat on a lake, sailing across the water on a beautiful summer day. The wind of the Spirit fills your sails and carries you along across the tranquil and serene water with the waves gently lapping against the side of your boat.

You don't feel inhibited by everything else going on in your life because you are taken in by the beauty and freedom of the day. You are at peace. Whatever worries normally crowd your consciousness have faded, and you are captivated and at rest in the glory of God's creation.

Now imagine that the water quickly drains out of the lake, and hidden things begin to emerge. An old, rusted-out car is slowly revealed. You see an old bike, a broken fishing rod, and other less interesting things that were sent to the bottom of the lake to be forgotten. Your boat strikes a rock, and it appears that your perfect day is ruined. Stuck in mud, what was once an experience of life and freedom now feels like being trapped and going nowhere.

These two experiences mirror what Christians have called "consolation" and "desolation." What we don't realize about consolation—as we are in the midst of it—is that the pleasure and excitement of the Lord lifts us from experiencing the brokenness and sinfulness of our souls. Like the day on the lake, the consolation of the Lord releases us to be driven along freely by the Spirit. This is an incredible gift! We hear a sermon, and even if it is a really hard word to hear, naming the very things we struggle with, there is a deep and abiding "Yes!" in our souls. This allows us to freely embrace the call of obedience. If the sermon exposes our failures, we don't despair because in this moment of consolation, we are carried along by the wind and the waves of God's pleasure. Our failure is not a place to despair but an opportunity to seek the Lord and know his faithfulness. We may know what lies beneath the surface of our lives, or we might not, but that is far from our mind as we are swept up in the Spirit's consolation.

When consolation fades—like the water draining out of the lake—and the Lord gives us the gift of desolation (and yes, it really is a gift), things change. Like a good parent disciplining their child, the Lord allows for pleasure and excitement to wane. What was hidden in the recesses emerges. The truth of our character, and the pains and sinfulness we have internalized, come forth as we are being called into a deeper kind of formation. We imagine that the Spirit's work will always feel like sailing on the lake. When the water drains and we no longer feel the pleasure of his presence, we assume we've been abandoned until we clean up the swamp. This is the problem so many Christians find debilitating.

There is, however, a different way to understand what happens when the water level decreases. We could look at things from a different angle. You are gaining insight into the terrain of the lake, and you are discovering truths hidden beneath the surface—clues to all that has happened before and how the past has given shape to the lake in ways you haven't attended to. If your focus is solely on having a nice day sailing, it will feel like your day is ruined. You wanted sun, waves, light, and the feeling of the wind on your face, and so the mud, junk, and rocks emerging from the bottom feel like the day is lost. But if you attend to the sunken car, the cave hidden beneath the surface, and the other oddities you discover, there are stories and wonders hidden all around you. If your heart is set on discovery, it could be that your day is really just beginning. If you are concerned with the truth, having it uncovered does not ruin the day but is an invitation into something more.

When the water drains, you are called into something deeper, and the Lord is revealing something more to your soul than you currently know. The Lord is illuminating what you avoid when left to your own devices, and he is showing you that these are not things to ignore but the path to growth in him. The Lord is calling you to himself in the truth of your pain, brokenness, and sin. He is calling you to a life of abiding in the vine and bearing the fruit of God's life in and through yours. This is your invitation into love—a love that calls you out of hiding to be known and embraced.

The only way to walk with the Lord is to increasingly see the truth of our sin and brokenness and to lay these down as we embrace Christ. This is a difficult path to walk, but the Lord reveals that this is the path of love.

Gifts We Were Not Looking For

After the Lord showed his power to save his people by raining down plague after plague after plague on the Egyptians, he walked them into the desert to experience hunger and thirst. Just like the lake draining, Israel never expected this. What we see throughout Scripture is that, along with the highs of consolation and the lows of desolation, there is something more mundane that can be just as confusing as desolation: the desert. The desert isn't necessarily bad, but it is dry, maybe boring, and it brings a sense of aridness to our spiritual lives. It is often in the desert that we first begin to wonder if something has gone wrong in our life with the Lord. In the desert, we begin thinking, *Is this all there is?*

The desert is where God leads his people to show them what is in their hearts (Deut. 8:2). Just as Israel was delivered from Egypt, the land of slavery and death, we too are delivered from the place of darkness and transferred into the kingdom of Christ (Col. 1:13). Like Israel, we see the Lord's profound work of salvation, and like Israel, we too are ushered into the desert to experience spiritual hunger and thirst. Like Israel, the Lord tests us in the desert to reveal the ways our hearts turn back to Egypt (Acts 7:39). Our call in this testing is to turn to Christ.

The questions we are considering in this book concern the Lord's work in all these experiences. What is the Lord doing in consolation, when everything seems wonderful and we are filled with excitement and spiritual pleasure? What is the Lord doing in the desert, when things feel dry and boring, and we wonder why things don't work well anymore? What is the Lord doing in desolation, when it suddenly feels like he has abandoned us, and the Christian life no longer works at all? What is God doing when he seems absent from our lives?

What we discover is that all these experiences are gifts from the Lord. The gift of consolation is an amazing gift, but if we don't understand what it is, we will fail to understand what the Lord is teaching us. The desert and desolation are also gifts, even if we would never choose them on our own.

We couldn't see this, which is what led us into years of confusion. After trying to fix our lives in the desert and trying everything we could think of to get out of desolation, we learned the Lord refuses to leave our sin, brokenness, and pain at the bottom of the lake. The Lord invites us into these things so that we can know his grace, forgiveness, and healing.

You have been called to deeper things than you may know, but they are along a path that you may have convinced yourself is wrong, dangerous, or even faithless. Like the disciples walking to the cross, your gut might be telling you that this path is the wrong one. Like Peter, you might rebuke Jesus for leading you here (Mark 8:31–32). But this is the path of life. This is where transformation is found. God is with you every step of the way, even when that path meanders through the valley of death (see Ps. 23:4).

In the first section of this book, we explore the ways we need to unlearn our assumptions about growth. Many of our assumptions lead us away from God rather than to him. Many of our assumptions lead us to rely on human-centered understandings of growth, or *fleshly* understandings of growth (as the Bible would say). The second section focuses on how these human-centered assumptions lead to a self-willed spirituality. This section calls us to unlearn our self-constructed visions of growth and refocus our hearts on Christ. To grow in the Lord we need to see the ways we avoid God, even in our spiritual lives. The final section is a call to walk the path of love with the God of love who has called you to himself.

Along the way we ask that you not only read and think but take what you are reading and thinking to the Lord to offer your heart to him. Allow your life and struggles to become the content of your prayer. Use these concluding sections to be with your God in the truth of your life, trusting that when he shows you your heart, that is an invitation to make him your refuge and to know him as your strength.

EXPERIENCE

Before turning to the reality of our growth in the Spirit, it is important to pause and consider what your life with God has been. But you shouldn't just ponder these things by yourself. We want you to think about them and ponder them *with the Lord*. Spend some time with the Lord and ask him to reveal to you the truth of what your life with him has been and how you have interpreted it.

Take some time to slowly read Mark 8:27–33, and consider the confusion Peter must have felt. Peter had assumed Jesus would act like the Messiah he was expecting. But now he stood before Jesus and had to hear Jesus call him Satan because he was living according to the flesh (setting his mind on the "things of man"). In the end, Jesus would erode Peter's presuppositions and prove to be much more than Peter could have ever imagined.

Open your heart to the Lord and consider the ways he has led you that you didn't understand, or maybe still don't understand. Have you wondered why God didn't "show up" the way you longed for him to? Have you struggled with why you feel so alone, when you are told that God is always with you? Draw near to your Lord and speak the truth of your heart to him, holding these things to him as you pray, *Lord, how have my experiences of the Christian life—both positive and negative—shaped me and my expectations?*

Ask him:

❖ *Lord, how did I understand the seasons of joy and excitement that I've known in my life with you? What did I think was going on and who or what did I think was responsible for this positive experience?*

❖ *How did I interpret seasons of dryness, frustration, and struggle, where I seemed to lose the excitement I used to have? What did I do when I experienced these things? Why? What were the deep beliefs of my heart about what was going on?*

❖ *Did I think I was the one responsible for consolation or desolation? Or did I know that you were leading me into these seasons to draw me close to you?*

Right now, pause and draw near to your Lord. Talk to him about your life and ask him to illumine to you what he has been doing in these seasons.

21

SECTION 1

Unlearning Assumptions About Growth

2

God's Path of Growth

Kyle and I both experienced incredible joy and excitement in our early years in the faith. God, the church, and Christianity were all painted in bright colors. The things of the world became dim and uninteresting. We were captivated, overjoyed, and filled with a kind of zeal we thought would fuel the rest of our lives. That was our mistake. We were young in the faith, and in our immaturity, we often equated passion with wisdom, excitement with depth, and energy with devotion. Then, seemingly out of nowhere, it all seemed to fade.

What became clear much later, that I doubt I could have understood in my youth, was that as a young Christian my heart was chaotic and driven by a focus on myself and on pleasure. It didn't feel that way to me at the time because I was finding my pleasure in the things of God. In his kindness, the Lord filled me with spiritual pleasure that lifted me up above the broken things in my soul. Like sailing on the lake, I didn't notice all that was under the surface. I was captivated instead by joy. So I didn't bother looking at the chaos, self-centeredness, and pleasure-seeking that defined much of my heart. In my spiritual youth, the one thing I knew for certain was that the Lord was at work in my life.

In those early years I knew God's presence and power and that he was present to me. I knew those things like I know I am alive. It was easy in those days because everything I gave myself to, whether church, Bible study, prayer, praise, or service, brought incredible joy to me. These were like conduits of consolation. God's grace was palpable. As I gave myself to all this, however, I began to internalize a kind of equation of the spiritual life in my heart. This equation was something like "When I read the Word, when I study, when I praise, then God comes." I did not yet see that I was developing a kind of "input" and "output" sort of spirituality. I didn't recognize the deeper assumptions being formed in my soul. There were hidden beliefs I couldn't see that told me when I did these things, I was tethering God to myself. I was securing his presence. I was making this happen. I was causing things to work. I thought I was the one securing joy through my efforts.

This same belief told me to look at my joy, excitement, and pleasure to know that he is present with me. I equated God with my experience of consolation. I secretly began to measure the presence of God by how it felt, by my feelings. This led me to misunderstand what God was doing in my life, and oddly, it trained me to avoid God in the very places I was seeking to find him. Discovering the truth of what God was doing in consolation changed everything for me. In understanding the Lord's work, I came to know a love that transformed my soul.

The Gift of Consolation

I (Kyle) grew up in a church that focused on emotional praise and worship, so I came to believe that if I really "showed up" in my praise and worship of God, my excitement and zeal would continue to grow exponentially. Other churches may be more voluntaristic, studious, or experiential, but the same sort of equations tend to be internalized. We come to believe that if we just do these things in the right way, then consolation will be the result.

Conflating the Spirit's work, consolation, and our spiritual practices is one of the main mistakes of our spiritual childhood. When we do so, we assume the Spirit doesn't work unless we passionately devote ourselves to doing those things. When things stop being exciting or when reading the Bible feels boring, worship seems dry, and ministry seems empty, we struggle with why the equation didn't work. Typically, and perhaps most obviously, we turn to ourselves, thinking, *Well, it can't be God's fault, so I guess I'm not doing this as well as I should be.* So we try harder. We throw ourselves deeper into whatever it is we have equated with the Spirit's activity and pray that it will work again. For many, the years of their spiritual adolescence feel like they are spinning and wandering. The Christian life that used to make so much sense no longer does. In pride, we came to think that it was our actions and the strength of our intentions to be faithful that secured God's work. We were still assuming we were the authors of our faith.

In my own life, spirituality was often tied to an emotional high, and I was frequently tossed by the waves of my experiences. When I went to Bible college, that all changed, but not necessarily for the better. When our original equations for life with God fail us, one temptation is to just replace one factor with a new one (or a new church) instead of calling into question the equation itself. So I just replaced my emotional high with knowledge. I grew, but my growth was still the growth of a spiritual infant. I grew in knowledge but not wisdom. I became puffed up because I equated passion with maturity, and my devotion became more of a mask for my sin than an act that led me to the Lord.

In all this, it is important to remember that consolation is a gift. The danger for older Christians who have walked through the desert and into their brokenness, pain, and sin in deeper ways is that they can sometimes look back at this season of consolation as if it was superficial. It isn't. It is in and through these experiences that we receive a deep foundation of intimacy, joy, and love. The whole of life is one long lesson in love; it is a journey in which the soul finds its rest in the love of God and neighbor. Love is the business of life, and it is the true transforming power of the heart. *This is what the Lord is teaching us!* Even as the Spirit groans within the deep place of our souls, we too groan as we await our adoption and long for spiritual freedom and happiness (Rom. 8:23, 26).

The Story of Spiritual Infancy

What is the Lord teaching us in consolation, and why is this his method of maturation? The Lord provides early consolation for the same reason we give a baby a bottle when they cry and hold them close in their distress. A baby crying out knows they need something, even if they don't know what they need. We give them the bottle to nourish them, and we hold them close to comfort them in intimacy. This meets them precisely where they are in their longings. But something has gone terribly wrong if a fifteen-year-old is drinking from a bottle. As the apostle Paul writes, "But I, brothers and sisters, could not address you as spiritual people, but as people of the flesh, as infants in Christ. I fed you with milk, not solid food, for you were not ready for it" (1 Cor. 3:1–2).

When a baby cries out for milk, we don't ask ourselves, *Does the baby deserve it?* As Jesus says, "What father among you, if his son asks for a fish, will instead of a fish give him a serpent; or if he asks for an egg, will give him a scorpion? If you then, who are evil, know how to give good gifts to your children, how much more will the heavenly Father give the Holy Spirit to those who ask him!" (Luke 11:11–13). The Lord doesn't wait until you have become an adult in the faith to give you good gifts any more than a parent of an infant would limit milk consumption because the baby isn't growing well or learning enough! In our initial immaturity, the Lord floods us with pleasure because that is exactly what we need.

The pleasure the Lord offers his children is a profound gift. It is a gift that we do not deserve, of course, because in this season of infancy we do not yet have the character in the Spirit to sustain an abiding life. In this sense, the pleasure the Lord gives in this season is not in keeping with our character but is in spite of it. We were infants crying out and the Lord gave us the bottle of spiritual pleasure to sustain us. This is a gift, but it is a gift that ends up leaving many confused when it is time to be weaned. If we don't understand the Lord's parenting, we will inevitably misunderstand consolation and misinterpret the desert and desolation.

One of the reasons churches struggle with spiritual growth is that they seldom think about the Christian life developmentally. We do a good job thinking developmentally when it comes to children. We recognize that children need different books and different levels of experience and teaching than adults. But when it comes to the Christian life, we fail to consider how the Lord matures a soul. In contrast, Paul recognizes that different seasons of maturity require different kinds of instruction and care. We know an infant requires different attention than a teenager does, but when it comes to the spiritual life, we seem to forget. In 1 Corinthians 3, the milk given to the Corinthians is teaching they can receive in their immaturity. Paul imitates God in meeting people where they are developmentally, even though he tells them they should be in a different place. He gives them milk because that is what they can receive. The goal, however, is maturity: moving from milk to solid food.

In maturity we can find joy and meaning in things we never would have imagined in our childhood. There is a depth available in maturity that offers a longer-lasting satisfaction of soul. Like a marriage that has worked through struggle, growth, and difficulties that is now basking in new depths of intimacy, the Lord wants us to know his grace, mercy, and kindness in increasing degrees. But this is only available through walking with him in the truth. In the experience of being weaned we can't see this, but the Lord really does have better things for us.

In our youth, the Lord gives us something easily digestible—because our heart calls out like a baby's cry— yet we don't have the maturity to embrace the solid food of deeper teaching and experiences of the faith. This leads us to an axiom about living in the Spirit concerning this early season of the Christian life:

The degree to which you lived by pleasure before conversion is the degree to which God will give you the pleasure of consolation in the early years of faith.

Whether we grew up in the church or became Christians later in life, God does not ignore our self-centered pleasure-seeking, *but he meets us exactly where we are when we come to him.* Isn't that incredible and gracious? God sees our pleasure-seeking and fills us with his Spirit in that very place. The Spirit of God, interceding from the depths of our souls (Rom. 8:26), pouring love into our hearts (Rom. 5:5), and bearing witness with our spirits (Rom. 8:16), meets us precisely where we need him. The Spirit comes to us as love, acceptance, and pleasure, such that in our conversion we can pray with the psalmist, "Like a weaned child with its mother; like a weaned child is my soul within me" (Ps. 131:2). God is not afraid of giving us what we need, even if it looks like pampering. He knows the way to lead us to better things.

Like infants in the faith, babies are little sponges. They soak up love, pleasure, milk, and everything their little hearts and bodies need. Infancy is a profound season of growth because intimacy, love, and presence are being infused into their hearts and bodies. Similarly, the Lord infuses presence, love, and intimacy into our hearts and lives in early consolation. In this season we know a Father who fawns over us. We know a God who rejoices over us in his gladness, who quiets us in his love, and who exults over us in singing (Zeph. 3:17).

It is important that we never look down on this early season of consolation. Spiritual infancy establishes bonds of love and trust, where God reveals his care, concern, and kindness. Jesus shepherds us in distinct ways in our spiritual infancy, just as he showed the disciples many miracles and even raised Lazarus from the dead before walking the confusing way to the cross. It is this intimacy and care that allows us to know his presence and faithfulness when he leads us into the desert and especially into desolation.

Finding a New Filling

When I (John) was a teenager, pleasure fueled my life. My life was driven by alcohol, sports, and marijuana. But when

I found Jesus, the Lord met me in my love for pleasure and immediately moved me to new objects of my desire. Suddenly, reading the Word, praying, studying, hearing sermons, and going to church filled me. God accommodated himself to me—meeting me pleasure for pleasure—to love him in and through this pleasure. But this is an immature love. He was wooing me to grasp him deeper and deeper, but I didn't understand that this was a developmental journey. I thought this just was what the Christian life would always be. The Lord had more for me than I would have accepted in my immaturity. Interestingly, Kyle had a very similar experience, even though he grew up in the church, didn't drink or do drugs, and yet still ended up fueling his life in and through pleasure, selfishness, and excitement.

God's work to mature us is often contrary to both our expectations and our earlier experiences, which is exactly why we fight against it. We kick and scream against being weaned because it is not the kind of growth we expect. We imagine that God will just take away the brokenness and sinfulness of our souls. Once again, God confounds expectations and offers a deeper and more transformative path.

Consider a person who has been filled with anger. When he becomes a Christian, it seems like God has healed his anger. It is gone. At least it appears that way. The reality is that God has filled him with his love, presence, and pleasure and has so lifted him on the waves of the Spirit that he is no longer mired in the realities of his sin and brokenness. He is given the gift of a season captivated by greater things. But what resides beneath the surface hasn't gone away. The structures of anger and vices of the heart have not disappeared. His character is not yet transformed. Many Christians end up despairing later in life because the vices they think they left behind seem to have returned. The day at the lake is ruined, they think, when in reality, the Lord is inviting them into deeper intimacy with him to transform them fully.

The surprising experience of growth in the Lord is that he wants us to see and know the truth of our hearts so that we can know and love him in reality. This is surprising because it is so different from what those early years of faith felt like. In fact, those earlier years *felt* more meaningful to a certain degree. Just as the mountain of transfiguration felt more meaningful to the disciples than falling asleep watching Jesus pray or journeying with him to the cross, the Lord leads us to abide in him in the desert and desolation so that we can grow in love. It is a surprising path, but it is also the path the Lord continually takes us on. This isn't new and is exactly what we see in Scripture, yet we still end up shocked by it.

Losing Pleasure to Find It

When Jesus warns that if we try to save our lives, we will lose them, but if we lose them for his sake, we will find them (Matt. 16:25), we see the shape of our calling. The early pleasure the Lord offers becomes the warm blanket that tells us things are going well. But the Lord is calling us to lay it down, just as he asked Abraham to lay down his beloved son (Gen. 22:2). What feels like loss is actually the path to life.

This is why many struggle with Jesus today, just as they did in his earthly ministry. They miss the fact that Jesus is not a plan for growth but that he is calling us to walk with him and learn faith by his side. Hear this: You have to choose. You have to choose to follow Jesus and learn that life is only found in him and with him. The desert does not appear life-giving, and on its own it isn't. But you are not called merely to wander in the desert. You are called to trust him. Let him take you by the hand and show you the truth so that you can learn dependence upon him. This is where true life is found.

The Lord's calling on our lives is clear: It is to know him as we are known by him (Gal. 4:9), to know his power in our weakness (2 Cor. 12:9), and to learn ever more deeply that without him we can do nothing (John 15:5). This is where life is found. But we must walk into these truths by faith or our experiences will blind us to what God is actually doing. As we are weaned, we need to learn with the disciples that Jesus is the true bread that satisfies our hunger (John 6:35) and offers the true water that quenches our thirst (John 4:14). We need to see the ways we fight against his work to lead us, however humbling a path that is. This is the way that leads us into abundant life (John 10:10). It is on this path where we learn about the peace of God that surpasses understanding (Phil. 4:7).

Fighting Against God's Work

It has become clear as we look back at our lives that unless God had turned our lives upside down, we never would have ventured into the internal chaos, self-centeredness, and broken realities of our souls with him. The person in consolation doesn't bother with those things for good reason. Our sin and brokenness lie beneath the surface of the water as we bask in the beauty of the day. The mess of life isn't the focus of consolation; it might even feel wrong or faithless to focus on the things we feel we've left behind. Importantly, this isn't a bad instinct. God gives us milk because we are infants in Christ, and that is what we were supposed to be. When the milk is taken away—and we find ourselves in the desert—the truth of our character reemerges, and things we thought we were healed from reveal themselves out of the recesses of our hearts.

As we receive from the Lord in early consolation, we are learning to attach to him, to commune with him, and to know him as life. The Lord meets us in consolation because this establishes deep bonds of trust. Consolation is learning to drink deeply from the One who gives us living water and to trust that by believing in him, we find satisfaction for all of our needs. Following this, when the Lord determines, the desert and desolation are the times when we progress in the school of abiding. These seasons are the call of faith to know the Lord and walk with him in the reality of our lives.

The surprising truth of life with God is that he leads us into our weakness, pain, and brokenness to reveal his power, healing, and mercy. Jesus, likewise, offers us forgiveness, not just once but as a path to increasingly see how desperately we need his forgiveness. This is why Jesus says, "He who is forgiven little, loves little" (Luke 7:47). We are forgiven in Christ, which is why there is "no condemnation for those who are in Christ Jesus" (Rom. 8:1). But because the goal of the Christian life is to love God with our whole heart and to love our neighbor as ourselves, the path we are on is one of increasing knowledge of how much we need forgiveness. To embrace Jesus's call into maturity, the path you must walk is one of knowing ever more deeply how needy you really are.

Invited into Love

Advancing in the school of abiding requires that we walk into and through our false assumptions and expectations as well as the misguided notions we develop in our immaturity. In conversion we meet the God of love who so loved us that he gave his only Son. This too is confusing. This too links loss with gain and life with death. This too is where we begin to walk with the One who promises the presence of his heavenly

Father, even when he cries out, "My God, my God, why have you forsaken me?" (Matt. 27:46). This is a confusing path of love, but it is the path of the One whose arms are open wide to call us to himself.

The path we are on is a path of love—a path of increasing knowledge of how much we need forgiveness, where the Lord shows us what is in our hearts (Deut. 8:2). This is a path where the Lord requires us to stand before the mirror of his Word and really see the truth of ourselves (James 1:22–25). This is the path where we discover that abundant life is available, but it is only available to those who follow God wherever he leads. But our God often leads his people into the desert. Our God confounds expectations and leads us to see the depths of our pain, brokenness, and sin so that we will know his perfect grace, mercy, and love.

If you find yourself frustrated, fainthearted, or despairing when the Lord shows you your heart or reveals how much sin, brokenness, and depravity are still in you, then this is an invitation to know that Christ is your righteousness. We know where the Lord is leading. Paul tells us about his own journey with the Lord:

> I count everything as loss because of the surpassing worth of knowing Christ Jesus my Lord. For his sake I have suffered the loss of all things and count them as rubbish, in order that I may gain Christ and be found in him, not having a righteousness of my own that comes from the law, but that which comes through faith in Christ, the righteousness from God that depends on faith. (Phil. 3:8–9)

We need not despair when we see the truth of our lives because it is only in and through the truth that we are ultimately set free. It is only in the truth that we can continually discover anew the grace, mercy, and forgiveness of God. Like the Samaritan woman Jesus meets at the well, when Jesus shows us our hearts, we can delightedly declare, "Come, see a man who told me all that I ever did" (John 4:29). When we trust in Jesus, we know that seeing the truth is always good news because he is our righteousness (1 Cor. 1:30). This is why the path through the desert and desolation should lead us to shout his praise and bask in his mercy.

Ask yourself, *What would it take for me to trust that this is true? What would cause me to walk down a path into the truth of my sin, brokenness, and pain?* Are you willing to follow Jesus into the dark and trust that seeing your sin, pain, and brokenness is actually the path where life is found? It turns out that consolation usually doesn't lead us here. But something else will . . .

EXPERIENCE

As we wrestle through these things, the goal is not merely to think about them but to bring our life to the Lord. In this chapter we have attended to ways we equate the Spirit with our activities. Compared with the freedom of the Spirit, who, like the wind, blows where he wills (John 3:8), we sometimes avoid this freedom by trying to replace the Spirit with things we can control. Maybe that is going to church, becoming a better person, reading our Bible, or having a certain kind of experience. Instead, in this space, draw near to the Lord and present the truth of your life to him. Do not try to manage God or even your own heart but unfold your heart and life to him.

37

Pause with the Lord and draw near to him and tell him, *Lord, you have provided so profoundly for me. You have met me in your goodness, grace, and consolation. Lord, you are so full of mercy.* Now, open your heart to him and pray:

❖ *Lord, how do you meet me in consolation, and particularly, how did you meet me in consolation early in my spiritual life? What were you doing, and how did this encourage me? How did I experience your work?* Hold this open to the Lord, and thank him for this season if this was true of you.

❖ *Lord, when did I notice that the bottle of consolation was taken away, and how did I feel and respond to this? Did I work to get it back? Did I feel guilty that I wasn't doing the right thing and turn to my own resources to try harder? Did I just give up? Lord, what were you doing in all of this? What were you trying to show me? Lord, help me to open my heart to your work in me.*

❖ *Lord, in my life, have I sought to replace you and your Spirit with things I can control, judge, and harness? Have I used strategies to avoid what you are leading me into?*

❖ *Lord, I want to be open to whatever you have for me. Help me to see ways and places in my heart where I am not open to you.*

Spend some time considering your life with the Lord, and seek to name specific ways that you have struggled with his presence. Bless you as you draw near to your heavenly Father.

3

Wading into the Unknown

When the waterline drops and we find our boat stuck in the mud, we are being called to wade into the unknown. This is an invitation to a deeper way. As shocking as it might seem, this is a gift. But we need a map. We need directions. We need guidance. Ultimately, we need to seek the Lord wherever we find ourselves. We need to remember who God is and who we are by his grace so that we do not despair but trust in the One whose steadfast love endures forever.

For the Christian, God is always present. He is everywhere, of course, but the believer knows that he dwells in our hearts by his Spirit. We must remember, however, that we know this by faith. Instead, we will be tempted to try to discern it by our senses and in our feelings. In the desert, and even more so in desolation, we are exposed to how much we rely on our senses rather than faith. These seasons are confusing because it feels like God has abandoned us. In desolation it feels like we're trying to carry the Christian life on our own shoulders. It will feel like anxious toiling.

What we need to cultivate is faith that knows God's presence by relying on his promise instead of our current experiences. What does this faith look like? It affirms Paul's words to us in Romans 8:

> What then shall we say to these things? If God is for us, who can be against us? He who did not spare his own Son but gave him up for us all, how will he not also with him graciously give us all things? Who shall bring any charge against God's elect? It is God who justifies. Who is to condemn? Christ Jesus is the one who died—more than that, who was raised—who is at the right hand of God, who indeed is interceding for us. Who shall separate us from the love of Christ? Shall tribulation, or distress, or persecution, or famine, or nakedness, or danger, or sword? As it is written,
>
> > "For your sake we are being killed all the day long;
> > we are regarded as sheep to be slaughtered."
>
> No, in all these things we are more than conquerors through him who loved us. For I am sure that neither death nor life, nor angels nor rulers, nor things present nor things to come, nor powers, nor height nor depth, nor anything else in all creation, will be able to separate us from the love of God in Christ Jesus our Lord. (vv. 31–39)

If God is with me, and if nothing can separate me from him, then why don't I experience this all the time? Why don't we always experience the Lord's presence like Israel, who had a pillar of fire leading them? Why don't we radiate the light of God's glory like Moses did when he was in the presence of the Lord, when we have the Lord indwelling us? Why does our life often feel so mundane when we have the Spirit dwelling within?

When Paul reveals that we are transformed from one degree of glory to another, he explains that it is through the invisible glory of God in our hearts and not the visible glory that Moses experienced (2 Cor. 3:16; 4:6). God shines the light of his glory in our hearts rather than giving us something we can see with our eyes or experience with our senses. This light shines into the deepest darkness of our hearts to illumine the places we don't normally visit in our souls. God has called us into adulthood, no longer under the guardian of the law but the maturity of faith (Gal. 3:23–25). By faith we must discern his presence and know him as the One who has promised to be with us and never forsake us, even in the remote places of sin in our hearts.

Surprising Directions

When the Lord led Israel out of Egypt, he led them right into a trap. Or so it seemed. Hemmed in against the sea, with Pharaoh and his army bearing down on them, Israel had to trust in God for rescue. Similarly, when the Lord led Israel through the wilderness, he led them into hunger and thirst. This time, they had to trust the Lord for their daily bread and water in the desert. When the Lord gifted them land, he gave them a place surrounded by superpowers who hated them. The Lord called them to trust him. But all along the way, with Israel using just common sense, it seemed like the Lord was trying to kill them—and that is exactly what they thought! After the initial consolation of the plagues, when everything seemed to work, God led them into the desert. It was there that he showed them what was in their hearts and there that Israel began longing for Egypt.

When ancient Christians wrestled through the spiritual life, they saw those same patterns emerging.[1] They noticed that while they were young in the faith, they experienced an infusion of God's presence and kindness before experiencing a dry season where things were less exciting. Instead of being laser-focused on God and the things of God, they found their minds wandering when they tried to pray. Their passion for God seemed to have run dry. Significantly, their will hadn't changed. They still longed to be faithful. But for some reason the experience was gone. Then life seemed to get worse. It wasn't simply that their minds wandered when they prayed; now they didn't want to pray at all.

Unfortunately, instead of going to God with these things, they had an inner dialogue with themselves. *What is wrong with me? I should be farther along than this. I'm not what God wants me to be.* There is a tendency to turn inward in the desert and desolation because of a deep belief that we need to generate excitement and passion to fuel the Christian life. We come to think that pumping up our wills with excitement is the way to be faithful. We imagine that we need to collect experiences to fuel our activities. Rather than learning to rely on God and be open to his love in our brokenness, we want to buy spiritual experience in bulk. We look for ways to avoid faith so we don't have to learn to trust. We want to turn God's guidance into a formula we can follow on our own without having to walk by faith.

Often, the difficulty in all this is that Christians have internalized a deep belief about how the Christian life works. They start believing their will causes spiritual growth and experience. If they don't experience love, joy, and passion, they think it is because they are not willing hard enough. They assume that if they were willing the things of God with enough energy, then joy, excitement, and passion would be the result. So when these things are not experienced, the only answer seems to be that they have failed to be faithful. The desert and desolation reveal the belief we have that correlates our action, faithfulness, and goodness with having a positive experience. But few question these deep beliefs and instead begin to despair, and they wonder if God is present at all.

There is something here that should be obvious but is often unstated. When we first became Christians and experienced consolation, we did not experience excitement and pleasure because of our maturity. The pleasure of consolation was by grace alone. It was entirely based on the goodness of God. It was given to us by God ahead of our character, but we came to think it was because of our character. In our consolation, God filled us with pleasure to turn our attention away from the objects of our selfish desire and toward him.

God is a good parent who lavishes gifts upon his children, but he is also the Father who disciplines, guides, and corrects. When he takes consolation away, we experience a unique kind of discipline—a discipline that reveals what the Christian life feels like when we try to lift it on the strength of our character. In this season we are being shown what has always been in our heart and character but was hidden under the waves of consolation. God's consolation was ahead of our character, and now he's revealing our self-reliance and our lack of faith. This is not a call to try harder, but it is often interpreted that way. This is an invitation to abide in him, to know our lives in his, and to know his strength in our weakness. When we no longer feel consolation, instead of wondering how this too is a gift of God's kindness as he leads us into maturity, many imagine he is rejecting us.

Weaned for Love

When we parent little children, we often fill their lives with the things that animate them. For babies, it is often blocks, dolls, trucks, or some other toy that has captivated their imagination. Using things they find joy in helps them develop. When we are spiritual children, our heavenly Father does something similar. But instead of finding what we are already excited about, God infuses pleasure into things he wants us to love, like worship, Scripture, and devotion. The same pleasure and excitement we derive through our love of sports, romance, and bodily pleasure, he provides for us as we give ourselves to the things of God.

When a child grows, however, and her parents start pulling away toys and games and replacing them with homework and chores, there is a lot of kicking and screaming (sometimes literally!). But even in doing this, we often provide encouragement along the way to help fuel them to do things they don't want to do. As early evangelicals used to say, Christian formation happens by weaning off worldliness to embrace godliness. This is true. But weaning feels like failure or abandonment—like something being taken from us—which is often why we can't understand it.

The Lord is weaning us off worldliness and onto godliness for life in his kingdom. This is what God reveals as he leads us through the desert. He is removing the felt pleasure of the Christian life to unveil something of our heart. It isn't horrible, but it feels dry. God now thinks we are ready to see what our character has become and to find him and his love in the reality of our brokenness and not just in consoling, spiritual pleasure. This is an invitation to abide in him in our weakness, brokenness, and struggle as he reveals his power and steadfast love.

We do, of course, have a choice in all this. As we wrestle through our boredom with our mind wandering, we can either abide in him, or we can try to fix it with our own resources. We can either hide, pretending everything is fine, and try to fix our life, or we can tell God the truth, that we are bored with reading the Bible or that we are uninterested in prayer, and trust that he really is God, even in our badness. We can either seek to clothe ourselves in our goodness, or we can find his forgiveness where we actually need it, in the truth of our guilt, shame, and rebellion.

In the desert, God is testing us to show us what is in our hearts and to call us to him. This is a gift. This test, as with Israel in the wilderness, shows us how much we are still filled with ourselves and how much our vision of life is still ordered to the world and the flesh rather than the Spirit and Christ's kingdom. This season can be confusing, but it is the path to know how much we need him, so that we are growing in love (see Luke 7:47).

The Gift of Desertion

In desolation, something new is added. The desert only removes the feeling of pleasure, which is why things feel dry. In desolation, however, God is giving us an experience—just like consolation—but now it is an experience of absence. Now we feel abandoned. God isn't absent from us, of course, and our feelings are not the place where we should discern God's presence. Here God is revealing that we are still trying to live by sight and sense rather than by faith and hope. In desolation, or what many Protestants and early evangelicals called spiritual desertion, God is giving us a negative experience that feels like his absence. When God's presence feels like absence, the invitation is to trust him and learn to walk by faith and not by sight (2 Cor. 5:7).

We know that the Lord is purifying our motives, intensions, and desires in his love so that love fuels every aspect of our lives. That is clear throughout Scripture but perhaps most obviously in 1 Corinthians 13, which reminds us, "If I speak in the tongues of men and of angels, but have not love, I am a noisy gong or a clanging cymbal. And if I have prophetic powers, and understand all mysteries and all knowledge, and if I have all faith, so as to remove mountains, but have not love, I am nothing. If I give away all I have, and if I deliver up my body to be burned, but have not love, I gain nothing" (vv. 1–3).

The journey to purify our desires, will, and character is a developmental maturation of love with the purifying fire of love himself. We have to repent of ways we seek to use our flesh to live the Christian life. This includes strategies where we turn against ourselves and berate ourselves for failing to pump up our wills with passion like a coach at halftime. Included in these strategies are ways we shame ourselves into action and even fill ourselves with anxiety to generate activity. These are all strategies of the flesh, leading us to ourselves rather than to Christ for our healing.

No wonder this experience is so bewildering. Protestant spiritual theologians were particularly concerned that when people were in the season of desolation, they wouldn't find a good guide to help shepherd them. You can imagine what they might hear today, maybe something like, "If God feels distant, it isn't God who has moved, and so it must be you." Now, confronted with guilt, they assume they must be doing something wrong and that it is in their power to get consolation back. Even more so, many imagine that what faithfulness requires is to get consolation back. But they are doing what they've always done, so it just feels confusing. *This used to work*, they might think to themselves, *but now I just feel lost.*

Where Are You, O God?

Immediately, many of us will revolt at the idea that God would give us an experience of his absence. Surely God doesn't do this! What would it even mean for God to do this? In the first place, recall that God is not actually absent. He is only giving us an experience of how little we are filled with his Spirit in our character. So now he thinks we are ready to see ourselves as we have become. This is an opportunity to see the truth of our lives with God, the God who sees us as we are and loves us right in the midst of our badness and struggles. We are called to know as we have been known (1 Cor. 13:12), and this season is one where we are participating in God's knowledge of us. It still feels like God is absent, but he is intimately present with us and wants to console and transform us from within.

In the second place, it is easy to forget this was something Jesus experienced. We pray in the name of Jesus, the One who cried out, "My God, my God, why have you forsaken me?" (Matt. 27:46). We draw near to the Lord in his name, and yet we never expect that this prayer will be on our lips. We should not be surprised when Jesus's prayers begin making sense to our heart. But they won't make sense until we can pray them from the truth of our experience.

There is, however, another example that is more striking. The apostle Paul, in 2 Corinthians 12:1–4, narrates an astonishing experience he has with the Lord. There, Paul tells us that the Lord took him up to the third heaven, and it was such a profound experience, Paul doesn't even know if he was in or outside of his own body. This is quite a gift! We might think of this as the highest kind of consolation available.

After Paul is taken up into the third heaven, the Lord gives him another gift. This is what we are calling the gift of desolation. Paul tells us,

47

So to keep me from becoming conceited because of the surpassing greatness of the revelations, a thorn was given me
in the flesh, a messenger of Satan to harass me, to keep me
from becoming conceited. Three times I pleaded with the
Lord about this, that it should leave me. But he said to me,
"My grace is sufficient for you, for my power is made perfect
in weakness." (vv. 7–9)

It can be easy to miss the significance of this passage because
so much is packed into it. Paul was caught up to the third
heaven. Throughout my life I have longed to have these sorts
of experiences. I thought as long as I could have an experience like that, everything would figure itself out. Interestingly, though, Paul's experience did not heal his character.
Rather, this experience led him into places of temptation of
spiritual arrogance and pride, so the Lord provided a new gift
to him. This was not a gift he asked for, nor was it a gift he
wanted. The Lord gave Paul a messenger of Satan to harass
him. Desolation was a gift to open Paul up to his desperate
and continued need for Jesus.

Desolation is often the medicine we need, but not the one
we want, so it is not surprising that Paul begs the Lord to take
it from him. (We should always ask the Lord to take our trials
from us, even as we lay down our lives to his will over our
own.) Only when Paul understands what the Lord is doing
through this gift is he able to embrace it as good. So Paul
declares, "Therefore I will boast all the more gladly of my
weaknesses, so that the power of Christ may rest upon me.
For the sake of Christ, then, I am content with weaknesses,
insults, hardships, persecutions, and calamities. For when I
am weak, then I am strong" (vv. 9–10). There is a deeper and
more profound sort of contentment when we walk through
desolation. Through opening our hearts to the Lord in the

truth, and finding mercy in that place, we grow in faith. This is where our satisfaction in the Lord matures.

As Job famously declared, "The LORD gave, and the LORD has taken away; blessed be the name of the LORD" (Job 1:21). It is by embracing the Lord in whatever he gives that we walk more deeply into maturity.

Unfortunately, unlike Paul, we are often left wondering what the Lord is doing in these seasons. We are not given a glimpse behind the curtain of God's actions, so we feel like the psalmist when he prays,

> But you have rejected us and disgraced us
>   and have not gone out with our armies.
> You have made us turn back from the foe,
>   and those who hate us have gotten spoil.
> You have made us like sheep for slaughter
>   and have scattered us among the nations.
> You have sold your people for a trifle,
>   demanding no high price for them.
> You have made us the taunt of our neighbors,
>   the derision and scorn of those around us.
> You have made us a byword among the nations,
>   a laughingstock among the peoples.
> All day long my disgrace is before me,
>   and shame has covered my face
> at the sound of the taunter and reviler,
>   at the sight of the enemy and the avenger.
>
> *All this has come upon us,*
>   *though we have not forgotten you,*
>   *and we have not been false to your covenant.*
> *Our heart has not turned back,*
>   *nor have our steps departed from your way;*
> yet you have broken us in the place of jackals
>   and covered us with the shadow of death.

> If we had forgotten the name of our God
>> or spread out our hands to a foreign god,
> would not God discover this?
>> For he knows the secrets of the heart. (Ps. 44:9–21,
>>> emphasis added)

Notice that, for the psalmist at least, the experience of desolation was not punishment of sin. It wasn't what we sometimes call "backsliding," where our negative experience is directly related to rebellion against God and his ways. Rather, the Lord was leading the psalmist this way precisely because God knows the secrets of the heart, and he wanted the psalmist to know them as well. This was the same path that Paul had to walk, and it is the path we are called on to grow in faith.

In these seasons of desolation, we can often discover an exhaustion that seems to rest in our bones. We are tired. We are fatigued. We pray with David, "I am weary with my crying out; my throat is parched. My eyes grow dim with waiting for my God" (Ps. 69:3). It is here that we discover more deeply the true cry of the Christian heart: *Lord, without you, I can do nothing* (John 15:5). But this time, it bubbles up from deep places in our souls and is not simply our recitation of what we've been told.

Life Beyond the Desert

In the desert, without the experience of consolation lifting our will and without experiencing how strongly we desire to follow God, we begin to see our character more fully. But desolation goes farther. Desolation reveals that our goodness—the virtues we have cultivated and the fruit we see in our life—is veined with vice as well. Even our virtues and devotion are filthy rags (see Isa. 64:6). Puritan pastor-theologian Richard Sibbes compares this passage from Isaiah with Paul's claim in Philippians 3:8: "I count everything as loss because of the surpassing worth of knowing Christ Jesus my Lord." The "everything" that Paul names here includes our good works, says Sibbes, because even our best works are tainted with the flesh.[2]

What desolation reveals is often surprising. We are not normally aware of how much of our spiritual lives are fueled not by faith, hope, and love but by trying to pump passion into our wills or trying to guilt ourselves into action or trying to shame ourselves into right behavior. Or, similarly, how much we seek right behavior, hoping to relieve the guilt, shame, fear, or anxiety we feel. We can miss how much fear or anxiety animates our life with God. When early consolation wanes, what is often revealed are strategies we use to advance ourselves—using our filthy rags as ways to find stability—and we seek to rest upon those rather than upon God in his grace. This is what the Lord seeks to wean us from. Desolation is the Lord revealing the truth that we long to establish ourselves more than seeking life in him and with him.

Throughout both the desert and desolation, we come to understand what it means *experientially* that the Lord is the purifying fire (see Mal. 3:2–3). To walk with God is to live in the presence of the purifying fire and to draw near to the fire that "smelt[s] away your dross as with lye and remove[s] all your alloy" (Isa. 1:25). Being with God causes impurities to rise to the surface of your life to make themselves known. This is what a purifying fire does! Just as reading Scripture should cause the thoughts and intentions of our hearts to be revealed (see Heb. 4:12), so too does God's presence awaken the deep things of the soul. In youth, we imagine drawing near to God will only awaken passion and our goodness. What surprises us is that maturity requires that our impurities are made known and experienced so that we can increasingly realize how desperately we need him.

What seemed impossible in our youth we come to know experientially in our adulthood—we are at our most rebellious in our devotion. We see this throughout Scripture. Whatever God gives his people, from the temple, land, manna, and whatever else, exposes them to the truth that they want to use these gifts in the flesh rather than with God and for God. In Exodus 16:4 we see this with God's gift of manna when he says to Moses, "Behold, I am about to rain bread from heaven for you, and the people shall go out and gather a day's portion every day, *that I may test them*, whether they will walk in my law or not" (emphasis added). Or, more disconcertingly, in Deuteronomy 13, the Lord tests his people with false prophets to see if they will walk in his way or follow these blind guides (a test the Lord may be continuing today).

Our devotion, ministry, and churches, along with our thoughts, wills, and virtues, need to be purified of their vices and reordered in and by the love of God. Desolation is a season to awaken these things so that one will cling to Christ more and more fully, discovering that his love and forgiveness go even deeper than we imagine. But we only discover this as his purifying fire brings our impurities, sins, and pains to the surface.

Perhaps more than anything else, desolation reveals how much we are trying to live by our senses rather than by faith. Desolation unveils our subconscious belief that what God really wants is for us to just act like a good Christian would. Desolation forces us to see how we turn to guilt and shame rather than the Lord and his grace to fuel our lives.

Desolation reveals how we go to church because we want to get God on our side and how we read the Bible because we think we can tether him to ourselves. In spiritual adulthood, we have to remember that our foundation is Christ, and we only build what lasts with faith, hope, and love. All else is consumed by fire (see 1 Cor. 3:14–15), which is why the Christian life is one of being purified by God as we draw near to him.

Retraining in Love

Imagine a child loves school. She thrives in the routine and is energized by the praise from her teachers and parents. Her good grades confirm that she is a success, and her teacher's affirmation fills her with the pleasure of accomplishment. Now imagine that one day this girl wakes up in the morning and immediately thinks, *I really don't want to go to school.* She is bored. It isn't a horrible kind of boredom, but it makes school less life-giving than it used to be. As she sits at her desk, she notices her mind wandering to other things. Instead of listening or studying, she fantasizes about playing outside. At this point, what used to fuel her, like praise and success, no longer seems to work.

This child is now at a crossroads. Will she try to convince herself that her acceptance, value, and love are based on her performance, infusing fear, anxiety, and shame into her pursuits? Will she start thinking about how disappointed her parents will be if they discover she is no longer as diligent as she used to be? Maybe she'll meditate on the experience of receiving a bad grade, seeking to use her fear of failure to animate her devotion to her schoolwork. In school, sports, or even with things like dieting, we can often try to manipulate ourselves through guilt, shame, and fear in an attempt to pump energy into our wills. But something deeper is needed to fuel our life with God.

In the Christian life, we too are tempted to turn to negative things—things like guilt, shame, fear, and anxiety—to fuel our life and our devotion. Maybe you've even had pastors try to use these things to get you to volunteer more, give more, or just try harder. When we are confronted with boredom, fatigue, or dryness, it is easy to pump up our will with anything other than faith, hope, and love. These take time, and we often want quick fixes. So we shout at ourselves, shame ourselves, or guilt ourselves into action. These motivations are burned up in the consuming fire of God, but he offers a way that is purified by the fire instead. When the Lord leads us into the desert or desolation, he is offering us a gift of seeing the truth to transform what fuels us. We are called to do more than just what we imagine a good Christian would do. We are called to love God and obey him from the heart.

A Roadmap of Faith

We would all love a roadmap of our life with Jesus that shows us exactly what will happen. But that isn't what we're offered. Instead, Scripture and the Christian tradition tell us that we will walk through seasons of consolation, where the Lord lavishes his kindness, grace, and mercy on us in experiential ways that bind our hearts ever closer to his. But we will also have negative experiences that teach us to trust him. These negative experiences help grow our faith. Sometimes this negative experience is the desert, and things just feel dry. Other times we experience desolation, and instead of just dryness, we experience God's absence. It feels like he has abandoned us.

The roadmap we do have tells us clearly that our call is to draw near to him and abide in him in every season of the soul. The goal is to always go to Jesus. It might even sound trite. But it isn't. It is tempting to replace that with sophisticated-sounding ways to grow, when the reality is that we just need to abide in Jesus. That is easy to say but hard to understand because we are often blinded to the ways we avoid him. In fact, what makes the desert and desolation so important, but also so difficult, is that the Lord is using them to reveal the places in our lives that need transformation, when we interpret them as things to get out of or fix.

You might imagine you'll first experience consolation, then walk into the desert, and then journey into desolation. While we have no doubt that many will relate to this, things don't always follow this simple trajectory. Often, we move in and out of these seasons in various ways and with differing layers of experience. We have started with a simpler framework—consolation, the desert, and then desolation—because it helps clarify these categories. Regardless of how we experience them, we know the Lord continues to test our hearts, revealing what is in us and calling us to himself. How the Lord chooses to do this is something he determines. Our responsibility is to draw near to him, faithfully walking with him in this present evil age. Our goal is not to figure out exactly what season we are in but to seek to abide in Christ in all things.

The Lord has not hidden our call from us. Our calling is to offer ourselves to the Lord wherever he has us. He is not secretive concerning the formation we must undergo. Our call is to do "the will of God from the heart" (Eph. 6:6). We are to "flee youthful passions and pursue righteousness, faith, love, and peace, along with those who call on the Lord from a pure heart" (2 Tim. 2:22). This is the call to blessedness, as the psalmist implores us, "Taste and see that the LORD is good! Blessed is the [one] who takes refuge in him!" (Ps. 34:8). We are to seek the Lord wherever he has us, trusting by faith that he truly is our place of refuge.

Learning to Remain

Throughout the Gospel of John, we hear the call to abide in Jesus: "Abide in me, and I in you" (John 15:4). The word *abide* can also be translated "remain"—we are to remain in Jesus—and throughout the Gospel of John, we are shown how people fail to do so. We see many of Jesus's disciples abandoning him because he speaks a hard word (see 6:60–66). We even see his inner circle struggle, and when Jesus asks them if they are going to remain with him, Peter responds by saying, "Lord, to whom shall we go? You have the words of eternal life, and we have believed, and have come to know, that you are the Holy One of God" (vv. 68–69). This is faithfulness. Our call is not to make our lives what we want but to remain with the Lord wherever he leads, learning to grow in faith as we abide in him.

Through every season of the soul we must ask, What does it mean to remain with Jesus here? How do we abide in him through the desert when our hearts wander and we are bored and tired? What does it mean to abide in him in desolation when we are confronted with the depths of our sin and brokenness? Put differently, we can ask, What does it look like to walk by faith in these places? Ultimately, we must say yes to Jesus as he leads us through these seasons, trusting that life with him is the greatest life there is, even when we cannot see that with our eyes or find it in our experiences.

The goal of all this is not just to toughen up or to grit our teeth and get through hard seasons. Rather, the goal is intimacy with our Lord. The invitation is to walk with God wherever he guides. When we give our lives to Jesus, it is like saying "I do" in a marriage ceremony. We say it and enter into the joys of the honeymoon, but we also commit to walking through seasons of "better or worse" to grow together in love. In these seasons with the Lord we are learning that he is what we truly long for and that all our desires point to him. In these seasons we are learning that we were not merely saved *from something*—sin—but were saved *to someone*—to God himself—and are to abide in him.

The Lord's work of maturation is a slow path of spiritual formation where we often lose sight of the road looking for shortcuts. Tragically, we often avoid this path altogether, looking for other ways to flourish that actually lead us away from him. If our calling is to walk with the Lord, the great temptations in the Christian life are to avoid him by walking in the ways of the world and our flesh (i.e., our sinful or autonomous strategies to navigate life).

It turns out, surprisingly, that we can avoid God in our passion, our brokenness, our goodness, our devotion, and even in fixing ourselves. Jesus is the way, and yet the path we walk is beset with temptation to trade life with him for something else—not to remain in him and with him. Embrace the invitation to be with God in the truth and to offer your life entirely to him. Learn what it means to walk in the way that is "not by might, nor by power, but by [his] Spirit" (Zech. 4:6). Enroll completely in Jesus's school of abiding, and be open to seeing the truth of your life so that you can grasp more tightly to Jesus.

EXPERIENCE

The Lord's guidance of his people is often confusing. We are tempted not to be truthful in prayer, praying instead like we imagine a "good Christian" would pray. Rather than praying in fantasy, draw near to him in reality, because there is no other way to draw near. Don't try to pray like you imagine he wants you to pray, but pray to the Lord in the truth of your life. God works in reality, so bring your life to him in reality.

Pray Psalm 88 to the Lord, and lift your struggles, questions, concerns, and anxieties to him. Don't just read it; pray it and allow these words to give shape to your own prayer.

Open your heart to the Lord and be watchful of your heart (see Col. 4:2). *Can I really pray this, O Lord? Do you really want to hear the deep struggles of my soul?* Offer yourself to the Lord and allow his Word to guide you to him.

SECTION 2

Unlearning a
Self-Willed
Spirituality

4

Avoiding God in Our Passion

I (Kyle) had a friend in college who was often carried away by her sin. She would leave church convicted and filled afresh with passion and intention, but by Wednesday or Thursday her strength failed, and she found herself doing the very things she had sworn she would never do again. She didn't wake up wanting to sin, and yet she was overwhelmed by it. Her solution? She filled her life with events that would awaken more passion to the things of God. Looking for something like an adrenaline shot or attempting to caffeinate her will so that she could be faithful, she went from event to event trying to counter the sin that so often seduced her.

After initially experiencing consolation, she came to believe that excitement was the only way to be faithful. Following Jesus made no sense to her without it. Because of this, seeking to generate the excitement of consolation felt faithful, even though it wasn't. The very thing that kept her in immaturity *felt* like it was the path to maturity.

What my friend failed to understand was that her character wasn't being formed for life in the presence of God. She was trying to generate excitement because she thought that was the only way to uphold faithfulness. Ultimately, the very activity that felt faithful was life apart from him. The very passion she thought was faithfulness was actually a strategy to avoid God, an attempt to create a life in her own strength. She was trying to re-create consolation through her self-generated passion because the Lord had used consolation early to wean her off of her flesh. She never imagined that she could become the kind of person who wouldn't choose sin, so she traded that for trying to caffeinate her will with enough excitement to sustain her in temptation. Instead, she felt empty. Ultimately, her will wasn't enough because she was trying to will goodness apart from God (even though she thought it was for him).

When I looked at her life, I could see that I did similar sorts of things. It didn't look the same, but I gravitated toward things that would awaken my passion so that I could be faithful. I too looked for ways to caffeinate my will to do the right thing at the right time. I too imagined that the only way to follow God was to drown out the desires of my flesh by seeking things that would create consolation. Instead of growing in my character and becoming the kind of person who would not desire sin, I was pulled by whichever passion was strongest in the moment. Instead of drawing near to God and being open to seeing the truth of my desires, I tried to mask them by fueling my life with things I thought he would like. In seeking faithfulness I accidentally cut myself off from him.

The Strange Experience of Maturity

Perhaps the most confusing part for John and me as we grew in the faith was that when we felt the most empty and stagnant, we were being praised by others for our growth, faith, and service. The more we were praised, the more we seemed to see how sinful, rebellious, and disobedient we were. The Christian life began to feel like a ruse, and people's encouragement of us only made us feel hypocritical.

Then we discovered something unexpected. When we began to read stories of Christians considered sages in the faith, they all seemed to have a similar experience. Late in life, when folks started treating them like spiritual authorities, they saw their sin more clearly than they ever had. At that stage, they were more constantly confronted with their desperation for God than they ever had been. From that vantage point they looked back at their lives and had a weird experience; they knew they were more mature at this stage than in their youth, but it *felt* like they were better Christians in their immaturity than in their maturity. This feeling is important because it reveals how easy it is to misinterpret God's work in our lives.

One example of this is the early evangelical pastor-theologian Jonathan Edwards (1703–1758), often considered the greatest theologian and spiritual writer of early American evangelicalism.[1] Edwards was surprised by his experience of how God matured him, and he realized that he often sought a fleshly path of spiritual growth instead of abiding in Christ. As he considered the zeal of his youth and the passion that had fueled his spiritual practices, he later realized that he did them with "too great a dependence on my own strength; which afterwards proved a great damage to me."[2] Looking back at his life, he recognized that though he was zealous in his youth, his spirituality was fleshly and led him into arrogance rather than humility. He needed to discover that his sin and brokenness were far deeper than he realized.

63

Edwards wrestled deeply through how we discern the work of the Spirit in comparison with the work of the flesh, which led him to see how the consolation he experienced early on did not aid his discernment later. When he looked back on his life, he noticed something profound: "My experience had not then taught me, as it has done since, my extreme feebleness and impotence, every manner of way; and the innumerable and bottomless depths of secret corruption and deceit, that there was in my heart."[3] Edwards knew what the Bible said about humility, dependence, and God's power in weakness, but he needed something more. He needed *experience*. Only experience of his sin and brokenness could lead him into the truth of how much he needed the Lord. He couldn't just tell himself these things were true. He needed to come to know them experientially. His struggles provided "more experience of my own heart, than ever I had before,"[4] which was the very thing needed for him to grow.

Sitting with his life before the Lord, Edwards came to realize how naive his youthful spirituality really had been. He writes, "It is affecting to me to think, how ignorant I was, when I was a young Christian, of the bottomless, infinite depths of wickedness, pride, hypocrisy and deceit left in my heart."[5] It is after he writes this that he makes an astonishing claim: "It seems to me, that in some respects I was a far better Christian, for two or three years after my first conversion, than I am now; and lived in a more constant delight and pleasure."[6] In his youth, Edwards was arrogant, prideful, and deceptive and yet filled with passion, consolation, and pleasure in the things of God. In his naivety, however, he had come to equate maturity with passion. Part of maturation is unlearning how we judge our growth and learning to embrace what the Lord has for us in every season of the soul. But, as Edwards reveals, this is a confusing lesson.

John and I relate to Edwards's experience. When the Lord removed his consolation from our lives and activities, it suddenly felt like the lights went out. We felt like we were wandering in the darkness. We didn't know why our passion for the things of God seemed to disappear or why ministry felt so dead. We began to see how self-centered, arrogant, and envious we were—how little love we really had for God and others. We saw how much worry formed our decision-making. We began to see deeper fault lines in our hearts than we could see prior. This was a gift, and yet we experienced it as failure. Our solution was to drum up passion and effort to try to fuel our devotion, but it was these very things that undermined our maturation in the faith and our dependence on God.

A New Sort of Zeal

It turns out that developmental growth is not as simple and straightforward as we might presuppose, just like adulthood is not as simple and straightforward as it looks to children. Many assume that growth is a gentle and easy movement upward, but this is a spirituality divorced from reality. Instead, the Lord floods us with his goodness to nourish our souls for a journey that proves difficult. To walk this path well, therefore, we must consider our experience and perceive how the Lord wants to wean us off milk and onto solid food.

The way early evangelicals like Jonathan Edwards would often talk about this was by saying there is a difference between passion and affection. Today we use the term *emotion*, but this flattens our experiences too much. In earlier Christian accounts like Edwards's, the distinction between passion and affection was fundamental. Let me use an illustration. As a college student, I worked at a camp where we frequently built campfires. We would start fires with dried-out birch-tree bark that we could easily light with a match. It worked great to start a fire but burned really hot and really quickly. In fact, it would burn so quickly that it didn't even work as kindling. We had to use the birch bark to light smaller pieces of wood, which would burn long enough to light the actual logs on fire.

That birch-tree bark is the psychological equivalent of passion. Many Christians just keep trying to generate passion, so they throw a lot of dried-up birch bark onto the fire of their faith, which only leaves them feeling depleted and consumed. Passions burn hot and quick but do not light a life on fire. Passions feel very powerful, but they are thin and superficial movements of our desire. Importantly, passions are not bad in and of themselves, but they are not meant to be sought after or served. When they are, they do not lead to self-control or maturity but keep a person in immaturity.

We often think of passion in romance. Romantic relationships often begin with passionate attraction to someone. This passion is not bad, but if the goal becomes satisfying it, stoking it, and living to increase it, the relationship will never mature. Mature love needs to be established in and through affection. Affections lead to the integration of the whole person in self-control for a life of love. Passions do not. Affections lead us to love someone else in a mature love, whereas passions keep love in adolescence.

One way to consider how a passion feels, and how it works against you, is to consider the experience of the passion of anger. We even talk about an experience of extreme anger as being flooded with rage, for instance, because it feels like it is happening *to* you, more than *from* you. That is what happens when a passion takes over. Passions do not lead to a person's integration—uniting all the aspects of ourselves to live wholehearted lives—but to disintegration. We become less united in ourselves. In other words, passion is not what leads into wisdom, self-control, or thoughtful consideration of the things of God. Rather, passions work against your mind and will, seeking to set you on fire with uncontrollable desire. A life fueled by passion does not mature a soul but leaves it in infancy.

It is along these lines that Paul says in Romans 6:12, "Let not sin therefore reign in your mortal body, to make you obey its passions." Or, likewise, in Galatians 5:24, "Those who belong to Christ Jesus have crucified the flesh with its passions and desires." Passions often govern a lot of a child's young life. It is through their passions that we often awake them to deeper things, and this is a work the Lord does as well in consolation. But it is never for the sake of passion itself. Maturity requires that we learn a deeper and more abiding way of desiring. Passions are too superficial to govern and mature a soul. Passions should awaken us to a path of depth, sturdiness, and commitment, but they are not what guide us on that path. Rather than in passions, we are called to live in abiding affection.

Persevering Love

Affections are deeper and more profound desires in the Christian life. Affections are abiding movements of the heart that lead someone into being more unified as a whole person. Affections flow out of the center of a person, integrating their thoughts, desires, longings, and hopes. One's affections reveal the overarching direction of their life. Christians are not supposed to stoke passions but should grow in affection. It is not wrong for our affections to awaken our passions. That is assumed. Affections will awaken and temper our passions, whereas the passions seek to overrun and govern the affections. Passions are not bad when they align with your affections, but to serve passions, or to awaken them to drive your life, is to live against the grain of maturity.

Unfortunately, in Edwards's youth, he thought the passion of zeal was the litmus test for God's presence and spiritual growth. Edwards's early subconscious assumption was that faithfulness required a constant infusion of passion into one's soul. This fueled an immature spirituality he later recognized as fleshly. He had relied too much on his own effort to create a life in his own power, making him arrogant rather than humble. Because passion mimics the feeling of early consolation, which the Lord uses so profoundly, we assume that we now have to mimic this same experience to grow. But it is this very instinct that the Lord is maturing us away from.

When the Christian life becomes about stoking passions, it remains superficial, leaving the person tossed by the waves of their emotional experiences. In our youth, we were tempted to think consolation would never diminish, but when it did, we thought passion was the secret mechanism to make life work again. We have seen many Christians seek passion because it feels powerful only to discover it does not fuel a life that abides in Christ. They burn hot and quick and are often left more confused than when they started.

Importantly, the *affection* of zeal, in contrast to the *passion* of zeal, is not known by excitement, or even by a feeling, but is only truly known by how it perseveres.[7] An affection grows not through passion but by the movement of a whole life—body, soul, mind, and strength—committed to an object of love. True affection is a deep and abiding disposition of the soul that permeates the whole of a person and gives shape to everything else. We cannot judge an affection by how it feels in any given moment, in other words, but only by the shape of a person's life. Passions feel powerful, which is why they are so seductive, but affections are the undercurrent of a soul that form a character.

There were many times at camp when I would light the bark on fire but then watch it quickly fade without igniting the logs. But when I was able to get the logs to catch fire, they burned with duration and consistency. This, not the former, is the zeal prescribed in Scripture. Consider the nature of young love in dating versus mature love in marriage. We shouldn't be surprised that it looks different. Serving the passions of the flesh for romantic love, for instance, is entirely different from having a deep affection for another that awakens passion for them. The first is a life of immature and fleshly passion, and the second is an affection growing in love.

In our current cultural climate, we are tempted to believe that passionate love is the only kind of love there is. This is why it is so easy to equate the spiritual passion of our youth, stoked by consolation, with maturity and faithfulness. In response to losing consolation, generating passion seems like the obvious solution. This, however, will keep us in spiritual infancy. As is always true with the flesh, it is easier to try to cultivate passion than affection, just as it is easier to create churches that stoke the fires of passion than to awaken and foster affection. It is easier to keep things burning hot and fast than to settle into the deep and abiding affection of the Lord that perseveres. It is easy to assume that childish things are actually better than walking in paths of maturity that require a deeper sort of abiding.

A Path Beyond Equations

When the lake drains and we are confronted with our pain, brokenness, and failure, passion becomes the obvious solution in our flesh to hold us above and beyond the reach of those things. We try to flood our lives with passion in hopes of drowning out the brokenness, sin, and pain we don't want to deal with. We turn to our subconscious equations as strategies to buoy us against the waves of confusion, and our equation looks something like this:

> If I'm serving faithfully, praying faithfully, and reading the Word faithfully (i.e., with passion), then I'll experience feelings of pleasure and excitement.
>
> Therefore, if I don't feel pleasure or excitement, I must not be faithfully serving or praying or reading the Word.

Notice that God and his action have no role in this. It is all about what I am doing and how I can fix my situation. This is a causal spirituality—where doing certain acts secures a response from God to give us what we want. It makes God a kind of vending machine that dispenses gifts as long as I put in the right code and make the right payment. It ends up being all about me and my experience and not about who God is and what he is doing in my life. Generating passion becomes the solution to our problems when we relegate God to the sideline of our spiritual formation. So instead of longing for God, we long for his pleasure, thinking, *I just need to do this more passionately, and then I'll get God's pleasure back!*

For John and me, generating passion in our devotion and service didn't fix our struggle. The Lord was showing us that the practices we had been doing weren't the answer. But this made no sense to us. It didn't fit the equation we had internalized. We kept going to church, and we tried to drum up excitement about it, but we still felt the same. We studied Scripture and learned more, but we still felt lost. We were being given greater responsibilities in ministry, but consolation still eluded us. In this state, a new code was being etched on our souls.

When the original equations didn't work, we assumed that the sin we were seeing in our lives must have been the reason our passion and pleasure were so low. The Lord drained the water from the lake to show us what was in our hearts, but we interpreted this as a problem he wanted us to solve. In response, we adopted a new equation: *Defeat this sin and you'll once again know consolation; fix your life and life will work again.*

This is a dangerous place to be. After playing sports in high school, both John and I turned to the training we knew. Work hard. Dominate. Leave it all on the field. So we worked harder. We learned Greek and Hebrew. We studied Scripture and theology relentlessly. We got more involved in ministry. The more we did, however, the more empty we felt. We were incredibly busy, and we were dying inside. The more we learned about God, it seemed, the more distant we felt from him. For others, their chosen path is not intellectual but emotional. They go looking for more experiences of consolation. Maybe they leave their church because that other church down the street gets them really excited. Their time is spent looking for emotional highs because the day-in and day-out reality of following Jesus doesn't *feel* significant enough.

In times like those, we can't see what we are doing. We think we are being faithful. But in reality, we are using these subconscious equations to figure out ways to make Christianity "work." Instead, God calls us to himself. He calls us to walk in his ways and to trust him by faith, when instead we are often set on getting back the feeling we long for.

John and I wanted a simple way, when the Lord offered us *the* way—*Jesus*. Ultimately, there is only One who is the way, the truth, and the life (see John 14:6). Jesus was calling us to himself, but we had come to believe he didn't really want our *bad*, only our *good*. So instead of coming to him, we apologized and we tried harder.

The Goal of the Desert

We can't overemphasize how confusing this all was. Everything that used to "work" now seemed to fail. Everything that once seemed life-giving now felt dead. The things that had captivated our hearts and minds felt like dust. In this moment, we forgot the obvious: We could have told the Lord what was going on in our hearts. We could have prayed about these experiences. We could have come out of hiding and told God exactly what was going on and how we were feeling in our confusion and anxiety. Instead, we looked for ways to generate passion. Instead of turning to the Lord, we turned to ourselves and the strategies of the flesh we had learned in our spiritual youth.

The goal of the desert is to show us the truth of our hearts and lives (see Deut. 8:2). God's goal isn't despair and frustration, but he is calling us to himself so that we can know a deeper kind of obedience and a more profound love and forgiveness. He does this by leading us into places that reveal our broken and fleshly strategies and the truth of our character. In doing so, he is weaning us off ourselves and onto him. He is revealing that though we accepted Christ by faith for salvation, we are trying to build the Christian life on the shifting sands of our passion. The Lord is weaning us off this fleshly approach to reveal that he is our hope, he is our life, and he is the only true way.

This is not as surprising as it may seem if we think about it for a moment. Scripture tells us that the Lord disciplines his children, and his discipline is meant to draw people to himself, not send them away. In parenting, we often require children to do things they don't want to do (e.g., get an education, take their medicine, etc.). This is ultimately for their good, but they struggle to see it. Similarly, our problem is not that God's method of growth is difficult to understand as much as it just *feels* disorienting. When we are confronted with this feeling of disorientation, passion feels more meaningful, and the flesh deludes us into thinking we can fuel our life with it.

The way of the flesh always leads us away from Christ rather than to him, and the flesh has no problem using religious and spiritual means to do so. The goal of the desert is to wean us off of these strategies of the flesh to know the firmer foundation of faith in Christ. But this requires seeing what still resides at the bottom of the lake of our souls with the loving Lord at our side. This is why loving much requires that we know the depths of what we have been forgiven. We need to take a journey with the Lord to know his forgiveness in the deepest places of the heart. This means we must be weaned off our fleshly strategies and equations, which are governed by what we can do and how much passion we can generate, and learn to abide in Christ in our weakness, pain, and struggle.

Relearning Our Calling

Imagine you are a child caught stealing a cookie from the counter when your mom isn't looking. As you eat, she walks in and gives you a look that cuts to your heart. Every child knows the pangs of conscience that swell in our disobedience.

Now imagine this is one of dozens of things you have done wrong that day, each significantly more rebellious than the last. When your mom tells you, "I forgive you for stealing that cookie," you are relieved because you aren't getting in trouble. But something remains in your heart, making it impossible to know forgiveness in the deepest recesses of your soul. Imagine, however, that your mother adds, "By the way, I also know that you . . ." and goes on to narrate every bad deed, every evil thought, and every rebellious inclination of your heart, *and then* tells you, "I forgive you." That is a different and more significant kind of forgiveness. That is forgiveness that comes with an invitation to draw near, be seen, and be embraced in the truth.

When we receive forgiveness in our salvation, we only superficially understand the depths of our desperation. We don't know the whole. We still judge things externally and have not yet grasped how rebellious and depraved our thoughts, inclinations, and desires really are. To follow Jesus is to have him take us into these things, not away from them. He takes us into them because he wants to reform our lives. Through his work, instead of turning to lust, we can turn to love. Instead of grasping ahold of worry, we can trust. Instead of seeking our own strength, we can long for his. The Lord wants to reform our lives in their entirety. To do this, the Lord reveals to us how much we need him, how much we need forgiveness, and how much we must depend on him for life.

If John and I could go back in time and walk alongside our former selves, we would try to help our younger selves see and understand that walking into our sin, pain, and brokenness *with the Lord* is the only possible path of faith. We would try to show ourselves that this is good news, even though we often experience it as bad news. If only we could have known that the Lord was calling us to seek him in all things—to come out of hiding and tell him everything—to know the growth that comes from God (see 1 Cor. 3:6), it would have changed everything. The experiences of our early consolation led us to believe that we understood the equation for life with God. As long as we felt passionate, we figured we must be growing. Let the Lord teach you his path of abiding, that you will bear the fruit of his life and learn dependence on him in all things.

EXPERIENCE

Instead of simply mulling over the ways you have tried to use passion, excitement, and devotion to tether God to yourself, we want you to bring all this to God. Instead of assuming you know the truth about your life, we want you to draw near to your Lord and open your life to him, anticipating that he can illumine things you do not see. Spend some time in prayer with each of these prompts as a way to draw near to the Lord:

❖ *Lord, reveal to me the equations I have absorbed and how I have used them to navigate the confusion I have experienced. How have I developed causal ways of relating to you?*

❖ *Lord, what are the strategies, beliefs, and assumptions I have internalized throughout my life? How have I responded to losing consolation (if I have)?*

❖ *When I look at my worries, frustrations, or concerns in my life with you, Lord, where do I turn? Have I been afraid to see myself with you, and have I just tried to change myself and do spiritual things so that I didn't have to see the truth of my life? Lord, what have I really been doing in my devotion, ministry, and life with you?*

❖ *Lord, lead me to know myself in you since you are my life, and help me not to be afraid of the truth. I want you to be my refuge. Lead me in your paths.*

5

Avoiding God
in Our Brokenness

I (Kyle) was a recent seminary graduate in my mid-twenties, alone in my apartment and in despair. I was trying to pray, but I was flooded with condemnation. I wish someone had led me to 1 John 3:19–20, where John tells us this can happen and that we should turn to the Lord who is greater than our heart and who knows everything. Instead, this fear and despair, rather than leading me to God, became a mirror to reflect my brokenness. It felt like I was cast aside and lost at sea. Instead of walking by faith, I felt it was somehow more faithful to try to fix my fear with my own resources. Wondering why God felt absent and spinning in confusion, I assumed God was waiting for me to figure my life out.

We have seen that the Lord leads us on a developmental journey of faith. As we mature, God guides us into different experiences to call us to himself and to grow in dependence on him. There are seasons of consolation, where he binds our hearts close to his in intimate presence and pleasure. There are seasons of the desert, where we feel dry and experience how much of our sin and brokenness are still warping our souls. There are seasons of desolation, where we can feel like we are abandoned and we have to see how much of our devotion is tainted with vice. Each season is a call to seek him, know him, and rest in the work he has done for us.

The path God has before us—the path of maturation—is always a path of love. But our experiences and expectations feel confusing. Our brokenness often feels more real than what faith provides, and our flesh tries to dictate how we should live. Being overwhelmed with what feels like failure can lead us into confusion and even despair. Unfortunately, without even being aware, we develop strategies to navigate this messy experience with God, often leading us away from him and back to ourselves. This is what ultimately undermines the work God is doing. Our call instead is simple: Draw near to the Lord in the truth.

Scripture tells us to draw near to the Lord in different ways, sometimes calling us to make him our refuge, to abide, or even, says the author of Hebrews, to draw near with confidence (Heb. 4:16). But this does not happen by accident. You can go to church, pray, or read your Bible without drawing near. You can do these, in fact, to avoid drawing near.

What makes drawing near difficult, in the desert and even more in desolation, is that our foundations become unearthed. It is true that Christ is the solid rock upon which we stand in salvation, and by faith we are his and he is ours. Praise God for the gospel! But as we mature, we come to see ways that our faith, hope, and love are mixed with other things. As we journey with the Lord, he reveals how much we have tried to prop up or fuel our faithfulness with guilt, shame, fear, and anxiety. But the Lord does not leave us alone to construct a life through our brokenness; he invites us into the love that can transform our shame into praise and our guilt into gratitude.

When we are afloat on the lake in consolation, it is easy to avoid looking at the mess beneath the surface. We might even believe it isn't there. We might hope, deep down, that if we only tack on spiritual disciplines, knowledge of the Bible, and ministry activities, we won't have to grapple with the struggles and pains of life. Instead, we must learn to do these things as ways of drawing near to him, being with him, and remaining in him. These practices are not life hacks to better our circumstances but ways we offer ourselves to God. These practices, furthermore, are not purified just because they are things we do as Christians. They are filled with good intentions, certainly, but they are also fleshly. So we draw near to the purifying fire and come to experience our impurities. This is an invitation to be seen and known and to offer ourselves to the Lord in the truth.

It is hard to see the truth about how broken, worldly, and sinful even our spiritual practices can be. But we can trust that the Lord wastes nothing. He reveals a deeper path, one where we come to increasingly see how desperately we need him and his forgiveness. This means we will all need to see how our brokenness is used by our flesh to prop up our lives. We will all need to see and lay down our self-empowered strategies to embrace the ever-present kindness of the Lord inviting us deeper into love. On this journey of love, our hearts are being purified, but we are also called to have our devotion, ministry, and praise purified.

The Nature of Our Brokenness

Growing up in the church, I had a good sense of what sin was. In the fall, Adam and Eve gave in to pride, making themselves the center of their lives, trying to be gods of their own existence. After the fall, this pride defines us, and to this day we continue to create lives of our own, generating strategies to dominate, win, or simply succeed and flourish in fleshly ways. But what I missed in focusing so much on rebellion was *brokenness*. Brokenness always goes along with sin. They are two sides of the same coin. They buttress and continue to beget each other. Because of the fall we are rebellious, certainly, but through the fall we are also broken, and that brokenness furthers our rebellion and continues to beget more brokenness and more rebellion.

As we grew in the faith, John and I focused on growing in knowledge, practicing spiritual disciplines, and engaging in ministry because we thought that although God forgave us, it was up to us to generate growth. In doing so, we talked a lot about sin but knew little about brokenness. This led to a devotion and discipline fueled by a desire to avoid the true reality of our hearts. It was a smoke screen to avoid the truth.

Too often in the church today, we pretend we can talk about sin and ignore brokenness, sending broken people to other places to seek healing. Equally tempting, however, is to talk only about brokenness without addressing the nature of sin. Unfortunately, there are few places in our current culture where we find people talking about these things together. But in Scripture they are united.

In the story of Adam and Eve, we discover the problem with both rebellion and brokenness. Their sin and brokenness are a mirror for us to see the reality of our lives. Rather than a flat, superficial reality, our sin reveals hearts that are desperate and fractured. When people focus solely on sin and pride, they tend to have a naive view of human brokenness, and their solutions tend toward self-help or quick, spiritualized fixes. They end up trying to ignore their brokenness and manage their sin. In the end, their brokenness, left untouched, drives their lives and seduces them into thinking they have inoculated themselves against the pride that still really drives them.

When Adam and Eve sinned, their souls broke, and that break continues to wreak havoc in humanity. Up until that point, Adam and Eve lived in harmony with God in the safe vulnerability of being naked without shame before God and one another. But in sin, something snapped within them. We are told that, suddenly, "the eyes of both were opened, and they knew that they were naked. And they sewed fig leaves together and made themselves loincloths" (Gen. 3:7). No one had to teach them they were naked. Rather, they experienced that something was wrong. Like children caught misbehaving, Adam and Eve knew in their experience that they were not what they were supposed to be. Filled with guilt and shame, they did what we all do in response: They covered themselves.[1]

In the midst of this experience the Lord comes into the garden. Adam and Eve hide themselves from God, knowing deep inside that they don't want to be seen. They hide because they are afraid. Once again, we see the human condition in sin. Fear and anxiety cause them to believe that God himself is the problem that needs to be managed. Like children who think the best way to deal with their sin is to hide it from their parents, Adam and Eve hide themselves, not wanting to be seen as they are.

Importantly, Adam and Eve's is not just *one experience* of sin and brokenness, but is the experience of sin and brokenness for all of us. Guilt, shame, fear, and anxiety become the strategies of a broken heart seeking to hide and cover to avoid being seen and known. Being seen and known in sin and brokenness awakens the deepest fears that we will not be received, embraced, and loved, and so we generate strategies of hiding and covering, managing and manipulating, thinking they will protect us.

As we grow, our strategies might become more sophisticated, but they are still strategies of hiding and covering. One might generate a successful career in order not to be seen, and one might hide behind pictures of a happy family on social media to cover the truth. It is not only easy but inevitable that we will use guilt, shame, fear, and anxiety as the way we fuel our spiritual growth and as motivation to fix our lives and energize our activities. In fact, this is what the flesh will demand.

With pride as the fountain and guilt, shame, fear, and anxiety flowing forth, it is no wonder that Adam and Eve are hiding from God when he shows up. When God calls them out of hiding, Adam tries to manage and manipulate. He subtly blames Eve and then reminds God that he is the One who made Eve in the first place, carefully shining the light of blame on everyone but himself (see Gen. 3:12). Notice what is beneath this. After sin enters creation, and Adam and Eve internalize the pride and brokenness of sin, God is seen as the problem. This is why Adam doesn't shout, "Thank God, he is here. He'll know what to do!" Rather, his response is more like, "Run! Hide! God is here!" This is like a child trying to avoid being seen and known in their badness and not someone who trusts that God is the path of life.

Ever since this moment, sin has tried to convince the heart that the path of healing is the path we must protect ourselves against. Sin seduces the heart into believing that God is not where we go with our sin, pain, brokenness, and rebellion. Sin whispers to us that God is the One we must hide from in our badness or placate with our devotion. Sin teaches the heart to hide and cover and to find another path, a path one can control and manipulate. Sin tries to convince us that we can manage and manipulate God, that we can do certain things to tether God to ourselves, to get him on our side to fix us, without having to grapple with the truth of what we have become.

This is why sin has never been afraid of religion. No matter what God gives us, whether it is the tabernacle, sacrifices, the law, or even the prophets, in our sin we will seek to use these things to secure God to ourselves so we can hide and cover behind our goodness and not be seen in our badness.

Begetting New Strategies of the Flesh

In the midst of this newfound rebellion and brokenness, Adam and Eve had children, and just as their sin and brokenness did, this reveals something deeper than merely the act of having children. Genesis 3–11 is not simply a history of human culture after the fall; it is the history of how sin and brokenness invaded creation. The births and experiences of Cain and Abel depict the strategies of the flesh, illustrating how our sin and brokenness beget a deeper form of hiding and covering. Human strategies try to manage and manipulate God, imagining he won't look at the evil in our hearts and see the damage we bring into his creation.

Cain, with a heart textured by pride and a soul saturated with guilt, shame, fear, and anxiety, killed his brother Abel. Cain did this because his sacrifice was not accepted and Abel's was. Jealousy reigned in his heart. Explicitly, though, we are told that Cain "was very angry, and his face fell"

(Gen. 4:5). In a broken and rebellious heart, there are two major strategies that serve as fault lines in the soul: anger and sadness. These are like sentries that our brokenness puts on watch to navigate God and others. Anger and sadness become the strategies of a person whose pride and pain seem overwhelming. Instead of coming out of hiding to know the grace and mercy of the Lord, we use anger and sadness to navigate life, often growing bitter, resentful, and fatigued in the process.

In our emptiness, we turn to managing our brokenness on our own. But in consolation, when we are so full of goodness, joy, and blessing, it is easy to think this emptiness has simply disappeared. Early consolation feels like a filling that has quenched the parched dryness of our souls. Likewise, the strategies of anger and sadness seem to be annihilated by God in the flood of consolation. But when the Lord leads us into the desert to reveal what is in our hearts, we often discover anger and sadness still lying under the surface, quietly driving our actions, thoughts, and desires. In the flesh, these become strategies we use to live life on our own terms. In the flesh, we just want to forget, ignore, and move on instead of dealing with the truth of our brokenness and sin. In Christ, however, our sin, pain, and brokenness become invitations to abide and to know his forgiveness so that we can love much.

The Great Lie of the Flesh

To the person who sees sin as simply doing bad things—and who sees the solution as trying hard to stop doing bad things—being confronted with this deeper brokenness can feel debilitating. This reveals how much we still rely on ourselves and our own strength rather than on God and his. This is why the Christian life can feel so heavy. We try to advance it by our own power. But we need him. We need not fear what we see in ourselves because he is our hope. Whatever you see in yourself—from sin, to pain, to brokenness—use as a way to lay your life down to him. We have nothing to lose in handing our life to Jesus; we have everything to lose by refusing.

As Christians, we are called to see the deep brokenness of our lives in light of Christ and what he accomplished in his life, death, and resurrection. This leads us to grow in dependence. But the depths of our brokenness and pain can feel like they are undoing God's work rather than inviting us into it. Many of us begin to question if God has been at work at all when we see unresolved sin and pain emerge from our souls. Instead of seeing our pain as the necessary path of healing, many of us assume that ignoring it is the safest bet, thinking it will just go away or not impact us spiritually. It is true that we should not follow our feelings, but we are to seek the Lord in the truth of our hearts. The attempt to ignore our feelings and persevere is a fleshly strategy of hiding and covering that continues to reign in the human heart.

Humans were created in goodness, love, and truth, and we were created to flourish in that goodness, love, and truth. But when the human heart is fractured by pride and brokenness, with guilt, shame, fear, anxiety, anger, and sadness at its core, everything becomes a temptation to hide, cover, and fill the emptiness with things we can control. Instead of being seen by God, with the fool in the Psalms we hope he won't look and see the truth (see Ps. 10:3–11). Instead of coming to Christ and trusting that only his robes of righteousness can cover us, we seek to use religion, morality, and success to cover ourselves. Even though hearing and reading Scripture should awaken the "thoughts and intentions of the heart" (Heb. 4:12) and leave us "naked and exposed" before him

(v. 13), we can easily read Scripture, hear sermons, and do devotions in an attempt to cover ourselves from his penetrating glare.

The great lie of the flesh is that our brokenness and sin are ours to fix on our own—and that this is what God wants us to do. Our flesh persuasively convinces us that we need to figure this stuff out *so that God can receive us*, leading us to believe that the Christian life is something lived in our own power. Instead of walking into the depths of the truth, grappling with how God has called us ever more deeply into his love, we try to stay in the shallow end of our life, hoping that if we ignore our sin and pain, they will fade away. This is what happens when we become convinced that God receives us in our goodness rather than in the truth. Convinced that God will not receive us in our brokenness, sin, and pain, we cut ourselves off from the only possible source of our healing—God himself.

The True Path of Healing

Ignorant of what drives us, we don't see the ways our devotion, ministry, and relationships are caught up in the lies of the flesh. Notice how James names the flesh in all its fullness and how he points us to God:

> What causes quarrels and what causes fights among you?
> Is it not this, that your passions are at war within you? You
> desire and do not have, so you murder. You covet and cannot
> obtain, so you fight and quarrel. You do not have, because
> you do not ask. You ask and do not receive, because you ask
> wrongly, to spend it on your passions. You adulterous people!
> Do you not know that friendship with the world is enmity
> with God? Therefore whoever wishes to be a friend of the

world makes himself an enemy of God. Or do you suppose it is to no purpose that the Scripture says, "He yearns jealously over the spirit that he has made to dwell in us"? But he gives more grace. Therefore it says, "God opposes the proud but gives grace to the humble." Submit yourselves therefore to God. Resist the devil, and he will flee from you. Draw near to God, and he will draw near to you. (James 4:1–8)

The passions of the flesh are driven by pride, which seeks to fill itself rather than being filled by God. These passions are fueled by the soul's movements of anger, sadness, fear, and anxiety as they grapple with the guilt and shame that texture the heart. When James names "friendship with the world," he is referring to what opposes the way of Jesus. The two attributes James names that define this rebellion are selfish ambition and jealousy (3:16). These are what define the passions of our life when they are governed by the flesh. This is an unstable life that looks to the strategies of the flesh to find stability rather than resting in Jesus.

This is why the "wicked," as Scripture calls them, have such misshapen desires. The desires of the soul, governed by pride but given shape by guilt, shame, fear, anxiety, anger, and sadness, warp the soul and lead the person to poison everything they give themselves to. This is why the psalmist tells us, "The wicked boasts of the desires of his soul, and the one greedy for gain curses and renounces the LORD. In the pride of his face the wicked does not seek him; all his thoughts are, 'There is no God'" (Ps. 10:3–4). In his folly, the wicked person tells themselves that God does not see. "He says in his heart, 'God has forgotten, he has hidden his face, he will never see it'" (Ps. 10:11). This is a soul textured by both sin *and* brokenness. We cannot name one without naming the other.

The righteous, on the other hand, are those who seek God's face. But the only way to really seek the face of God is to do so in truth (see Ps. 145:18). So the psalmist prays, "How long, O LORD? Will you forget me forever? How long will you hide your face from me? How long must I take counsel in my soul and have sorrow in my heart all the day?" (Ps. 13:1–2). Instead of pretending that everything is fine, the psalmist asks the Lord if he has forgotten him. In the desert, the psalmist wonders why God's face no longer shines upon him. This is the heart of one who comes to God to honestly share with him the truth of what is really going on in their heart; this is the heart that has faith. It is the very opposite of what we often assume being righteous will be like. This is the way of faith, a faith that takes everything to God without fear.

Faith and hope teach the heart that sin is a liar, and that the only possible path of healing is God himself. Faith and hope reject the lies of the flesh and take both sin and brokenness to the cross, trusting that the One who died for us in our sin is the One who can meet us there. By faith and hope, we hear God walk into the garden of our own sin and brokenness, and instead of saying, "Run! Hide!" we can say, "Praise the Lord that he is here! 'There is therefore now no condemnation for those who are in Christ Jesus'" (Rom. 8:1).

Blinded by Intention

Our response to sermons often reveals how the strategies of our heart lead us either to God or into hiding and covering. This is why it is helpful to consider what we experience when we hear a sermon. Many experience the intentions of being good and being faithful, and while these are the right intentions to have, they can also lead us to ourselves rather than to God. We begin to infuse passion into our intention to be faithful, but it too often blinds us to the truth of our heart. We can bask in the strength of our intention to be good rather than allowing that intention to lead us to the Lord in our need. We end up having an experience of strong intention, which we ultimately equate with God's "presence," and therefore miss the deeper rebellion in our souls.

Pause and think about that for a moment, because most are unaware that we do this. What do you do when you hear a sermon?

- ❖ Do you leave, thinking of ways to fix your life and make yourself more receivable?
- ❖ Do you look for ways to awaken your passion so you can be more zealous?
- ❖ Do you deflect a hard word from a sermon and focus on everyone else you know who needs to hear that word?
- ❖ Do you leave a sermon with a new piece of information you can use to further affirm that you are right about theology so you can post a quote online?

After consolation, it is easy to use our good intentions, and especially the strength of our intentions, to mirror our goodness back to ourselves rather than looking at our sin and brokenness. This is one of the strategies of the flesh to hide and cover—not only from others but even from ourselves—so that we don't have to see the truth.

We have talked about the "strength of our intentions" and "pumping up our wills" as ways to generate passion to advance ourselves in the Christian life. An image might help explain this experience. Think of pretty much any American sports movie. A team is down big at halftime, and the coach gives a rousing halftime talk, trying to wake his team up by infusing intention into their wills. He wants to awaken their adrenaline. He wants to pump them up with excitement. He is trying to caffeinate them into action. In the Christian life, we often do this to mimic the original feeling of consolation because we still think that exciting our will is the only way to be obedient.

When we hear a sermon and we experience a jolt of guilt or shame, we are tempted to think the faithful response is to awaken our will with a "pep talk." Trying to deal with guilt and shame by exciting our intention causes us to imagine that we can clothe our nakedness and that we don't need to be clothed with Christ's robes of righteousness. But God's grace beckons us in our guilt and shame. This is a call to stop hiding, fixing, and covering ourselves and to know God's love and forgiveness where we actually need it. Guilt and shame, in grace, are invitations to grasp ahold of Jesus to know his power in our weakness and not our own strength through good intentions.

In a similar way, one of the reasons many love highly passionate worship is because they hope that filling their intention with passion will carry them into obedience. It feels powerful. But passion does not transform our character, and when excitement wanes, our character emerges. Passion becomes the place we turn to so we don't have to see the truth of our character, because this feels like we're going backwards. But when we are tossed to and fro by the waves of passion, or other strategies of the flesh, we lack the internal stability to continue down a path of maturity. So many try to fill themselves with passion or right information on Sunday morning, only to discover their intention has worn out by Wednesday.

Because we often don't pause and really understand what we are feeling in our guilt, shame, fear, anxiety, anger, or sadness, we are easily governed by them. Instead of recognizing what is feeding these things or what they are fueling in our lives, we only know that we feel bad. These feelings color how we think and what we assume, and we often assume they are accurate messages about who we are, who God is, and what fixing our lives looks like. We might not know we feel guilty because we experience it as the deep sense that we need to work a bit harder and do a bit more. When we commit to doing more, this feeling goes away and we assume God is satisfied. Likewise, we might not know we feel shameful or afraid, but it appears in decisions we make or what we feel in our bodies. We might not admit we are angry people, but we might notice that we avoid God in our anger because we imagine we are not receivable in that place.

The danger with our brokenness is that either we tend to ignore it, missing the ways it guides and governs our lives, or else we accept our feelings as bare fact, assuming what we feel is the voice of God. We feel guilty and either think it is our job to make that feeling go away or assume God is making us feel that way. If we feel ashamed, we assume God is telling us we should be ashamed of ourselves and need to clothe ourselves in our goodness rather than receive his robes of righteousness. If we feel afraid, we assume God is holding us under his thumb until we get our act together.

Our experiences with brokenness are of fundamental importance because only the truth about who God is and what he is like can lead us into freedom. True life is found in the presence of the holy God in reality and not in the fantasy of our flesh. If you imagine God is bubbling forth with wrath, looking for you to step out of line so that he can punish you, you will never draw near to him. The test for whether you think this way deep down is if, instead of coming out of hiding and telling God the truth of what is going on in your soul, you seek ways to placate him through your actions or strategies to tether him to yourself. You'll try to domesticate God rather than laying your life before him.

God guides us to know what Jesus has done for us so that we can properly navigate our guilt, shame, fear, anxiety, anger, and sadness. Only the life, death, resurrection, and ascension of Jesus, and his current reign and rule at the right hand of God, can rescue us in our brokenness and sin. But we are tempted to turn to fleshly ways to fix our lives when we feel these things, and we are tempted to allow them rather than Scripture to determine what God is like. When this happens, we become tossed by the waves of our emotional lives, often turning to passion as the solution, hoping that if we're passionate enough about the things of God, then this tumultuous sea will stop raging. But using our passions this way only adds to the chaotic waters and leaves us, once again, feeling alone, empty, and confused.

We are sinners. We are broken. Our brokenness often leads us deeper into sin, and our sin begets deeper and deeper brokenness. Only the Lord can meet us here. Only the Lord can break this cycle of pain and rebellion. But we need to meet the Lord in the truth of what is going on within ourselves—and let him and his truth inform, convict, and forgive us in reality. We need to draw near as we really are so that we can receive him as he really is.

Your call in the Christian life is not to fix your brokenness. You cannot solve the problem of your guilt, shame, fear, and anxiety. But you can come to the Lord, who meets you in these things and transforms them in and through his love. If you try instead to fuel your devotion with your guilt or to use anxiety to caffeinate your will, you may construct a life that is impressive, but it won't be a life of love. Alongside your accomplishments you will find bitterness, rage, and exhaustion because you are using your flesh to buoy yourself. But only Christ can bear the weight of your life. Only Christ can meet you in the truth of your guilt and shame, fear and anxiety, and anger and sadness. Only Christ can transform the deep places in and by his love. Only Christ can expose you to your strategies to avoid him while simultaneously holding his arms of love open to you.

EXPERIENCE

The Lord calls you to boldly ascend to his throne of grace, not because you have life figured out but because you have a great high priest in Jesus (see Heb. 4:16). Intend, right now, to draw near to the Lord. Trust that Jesus has done everything necessary to give you access to the Father, so you can draw near in his name and not your own. If you wonder if you will be received, remember that it is only by faith in Jesus that we are righteous, clean, and holy (see 1 Cor. 1:30). It is only by faith in Jesus that we have access to the Father as his children (see Eph. 2:18–20).

So draw near and consider: What would it look like to know your fears and to open those fears to the Lord? What would it look like to feel your anxieties and, instead of just worrying about them, lay them before the Lord? Are there ways you can see guilt, shame, fear, anxiety, anger, and sadness begetting a kind of religion of managing and manipulating God or just trying to create excitement and zeal instead of leading you to abide in him? Or maybe you've just equated being excited with abiding? Draw near to your Lord and open your heart to him in the truth:

❖ *Lord, I want to lift up this day, this week, and this season of my life to you. Look and see every aspect of it. Look at the ways I am driven by guilt, shame, anxiety, fear, anger, or sadness. Lord, I want you in these places. My Father, I need you in these places.*

❖ *Lord, show me my longings. Show me how my pride, sin, and brokenness have led me to strategies of my flesh to try to manage and manipulate you rather than make you my refuge. Lord, meet me here.*

❖ *Lord, show me the truth of my anger and my sadness. Jesus, without you I can do nothing. Know me in the truth of these things. See how I use anger and sadness to navigate my life apart from you. Help me, Lord. Allow me to draw near to you in the truth so that I can know your love, kindness, and forgiveness.*

Sit with this prayer of David:

> Preserve me, O God, for in you I take *refuge.*
> I say to the Lord, "You are my Lord;
> I have no good apart from you." (Ps. 16:1–2,
> emphasis added)

Consider with the Lord, *What would it mean for me to make you my refuge? Help me, Lord. Help me not to make myself or my performance in life or devotion my refuge. My God, I want you to be my refuge.*

INTERLUDE

Losing Grip on the Gospel

Throughout this book, we are inviting you to enter into the heart of the Good News. This is important because it is easy to lose grip on the gospel. It is easy to start feeling heavy as we see how many of the ways we thought we were being faithful have actually become ways to avoid God. Do not lose heart! This is an invitation to come to Christ to know his love, forgiveness, and mercy ever more deeply. But these realities will be experienced differently in different seasons of our spiritual journey. In times of consolation, they will seem wonderful. We will feel the Good News radiate through us, even though it isn't consonant with our character. In later consolation, we will experience the goodness of God as our character comes to harmonize with him and his love. In either case, those moments will be filled with satisfaction in the sweetness of Jesus's presence and care.

However, in the desert or in times of desolation, the good news of Jesus takes on a new role as a mirror to the truth of our souls. In these difficult seasons, we rest in the gospel as an invitation to look into the mirror, as Jesus calls us to do, and not to turn around and forget what we look like (see James 1:23–24). What consolation spared us from, now in the desert and desolation we must attend to. The Lord ultimately calls his people to look into the mirror of the law and our disobedience and not to despair but to proclaim with Paul, "The law came in to increase the trespass, but where sin increased, grace abounded all the more" (Rom. 5:20). Grace abounds! This isn't an invitation to sin or to neglect your obedience to the Lord, of course. This is a call to draw near to him and grasp him and his grace with everything you have in the good, the sin, and the brokenness in your soul. This is a call to be obedient from the heart.

The danger in our lives, however, is that we can trade the gospel for something else, which happens immediately in the New Testament church (see Gal. 3:1–3; Col. 2:16–23). We start believing that we have been forgiven but now need to get our act together by using guilt, shame, fear, anxiety, or just our own ability to achieve and to guide our behavior. There is a danger, in other words, in thinking that the gospel has dealt with the former issues in our lives but now God demands we figure our lives out. There is even a danger in thinking that the gospel simply establishes a way—a path we can walk—and that Christ is a mere example to follow. The gospel, it turns out, is far bigger and far greater. Martin Luther writes,

> The chief article and foundation of the Gospel is that before you take Christ as an example, you accept and recognize him as a gift, as a present that God has given to you and that is your own. This means that when you see or hear of Christ doing or suffering something, you do not doubt that Christ himself, with his deeds and suffering, belongs to you. On this you may depend as surely as if you had done it yourself; indeed as if you were Christ himself.[1]

Luther, rather than choosing union over imitation, claims that the only way we can truly imitate Christ is by grasping ahold of him as a gift. He reminds us that we first receive Christ by grace, such that we are his and he is ours, and only in abiding in him are our lives conformed to his. But we never leave his embrace. The path to looking like Christ comes only through union and communion with him. It is only in abiding in him—grasping him as our all in all—that our lives are shaped like Jesus's.

Our invitation to you is to know that the Lord is your Shepherd who leads you into green pastures (Ps. 23:1–2) but also walks you through the "valley of the shadow of death" (v. 4) and even prepares a table for you in the presence of your enemies (v. 5). But he is with you. He is leading. He is your righteousness, so you don't need to fear the truth but can now see your failures, brokenness, and even sin as new opportunities to lay down your life to him who has given himself to you. Jesus's school of abiding is always taught in the truth because it is only there that we can grasp ahold of him who gives us life.

Therefore, if this feels heavy to you or you begin to feel hopeless, take heart and rejoice! You cannot bear the weight of your salvation or your growth. They are not yours to bear. You need Christ. This is good news to a weary soul. He is your hope and he is your salvation. Instead of hopelessness, see your sin, brokenness, and failure as a chance to place your hope fully in Christ. Remember the gospel, and don't lose heart. Hear the words of Jesus: "Come to me, all who labor and are heavy laden, and I will give you rest. Take my yoke upon you, and learn from me, for I am gentle and lowly in heart, and you will find rest for your souls. For my yoke is easy, and my burden is light" (Matt. 11:28–30).

6

Avoiding God in
Our Goodness

Although John and I had similar experiences of early consolation, we each experienced it differently because of
how we grew up. John became a Christian after high school,
so early consolation was deeply wedded with forgiveness of
his previous sins. It was all joy and excitement and growth.
For me, that all felt different. I grew up in a Christian home,
and all I ever knew were stories about Jesus and forgiveness
but also a deep sense of law and of God as judge. I didn't
have the experience of going from a lawless life to forgiven
in Jesus—that wasn't what it felt like for me—my experience
was being known as a Christian and failing a lot.

Lots of things factored into this, but I lived a very chaotic
early life, often driven by my passions in one way or another,
and spent most of my childhood in trouble. I knew what the
gospel said, and I knew that Jesus was Lord, but I struggled
with the idea that I could be received. I was overcome with

guilt. I wrestled deeply with fear and anxiety. Even in the joy of early consolation, I had a sense within me that I had gone too far. My life felt too broken and disobedient to be Christian. Confronted with the weight of my sin and brokenness, I thought God was demanding that I get my life together.

When I focused on being good and doing all the things I imagined a mature Christian would do, I was praised by leaders in the church. So I imagined that maturity meant pretending like I was good and doing whatever it took to fuel my life for goodness. But this didn't eradicate the feeling that this was only masking my condemnation. So when the desert hit, it seemed like a sign from God that I was rejected. When I found myself in desolation, it seemed like further proof that my life was a charade.

The only way I knew how to interpret the desert and desolation was that they were God's demand that I get my life together. Rather than these things leading me to Christ, they led me back to my own resources. So, even though I didn't know I was doing it, I was trying really hard to be good so that God would like me. If I managed to do more good things than bad things on any given day, I imagined his anger subsided a bit. If I failed, I waited for his condemnation. In doing so, I was tethering God to myself, hoping I could manage him through my goodness.

What I couldn't see in my quest to be good was how unfaithful it really was. I was giving in to a temptation to try to avoid God in my goodness. Spiritual formation is constantly confronted with temptations to take shortcuts or bypass the messy work of growth for something cleaner and more sterile. Even good books on spiritual formation, though they don't intend to, can provide directions for avoiding God in our goodness by learning spiritual practices apart from him. We have to name this truth and see how we are uniquely tempted by these things or else we will continually be seduced by them.

More disconcerting, perhaps, is how many Christians end up believing that the path of Jesus is *bad news*. They initially hear the good news of the gospel and think life will finally work the way they want it to. But then Jesus makes them count the cost of following him. He reveals what it means to follow the One who walked the way of the cross and calls us to bear our crosses and follow him. Now we must wrestle through all the ways we see this as bad news rather than as an invitation to life and love from the One who can offer it. Therefore, as we continue to wrestle with ways we avoid God, our hope for you is that a very simple prayer would begin to bubble up from your soul: *Lord, I want you. Without you, I can do nothing.* Find rest and peace in Jesus, not in your goodness.

The Moralistic Temptation

When consolation wanes, one of the most subtle and deceptive temptations is to reject the path of maturity for the path of moralism, turning to our own moral efforts instead of God when we are confronted with our spiritual failure and immaturity. Moralists hate the desert and desolation because it forces them to look at what they are set on avoiding: the truth of their heart. So they seek consolation to hide and convince themselves and others that everything is fine. In general, moralism is our well-intentioned attempt to use spiritual formation, spiritual disciplines, ministry, service, obedience, or just plain moral behavior to relieve the burden of our spiritual failure. Put differently, moralism is the strategy to do in the flesh what only Christ can do for us.

It is not hard to see that moralism is bad, but few recognize how deeply it has formed them. As seminary professors, we regularly meet students who became missionaries or pastors because consolation faded, which led them to believe God was displeased with them. They assumed the only way to "get God back on their side" was to do full-time ministry. Then one day on the mission field, while preparing a sermon or working in youth ministry, they realized their faith was on life support. God led them to the desert to be with him and to know him. He led them into dryness so they could see the truth of their flesh and more deeply embrace his grace and love. But instead, their response was to prove to him that they were good. They interpreted the desert as a demand from God: *Get your act together, and then I will be near you!*

Moralism tempts us because we assume it is what maturity requires. The problem, however, is much deeper than it appears. Moralism is the logic of the flesh, so it is not simply that some people are tempted by it—all are. All Christians struggle with moralism in the life of faith.

Trading the Spirit for the Flesh

It would be easy to write off the idea of moralism. I (Kyle) was once speaking at a pastors' conference on the temptation to moralism and I overheard an older pastor critiquing my talk. He said, "The speaker was warning against making people good, but what else are we supposed to do?" As he went on, it was clear that his goal in ministry was simply to make moral people, and so the idea that moralism was bad seemed incoherent.

But much of Jesus's ministry was a direct attack on a kind of goodness that was sought after instead of turning to God. In Luke 18, Jesus tells a parable about two men who go to the temple to pray: one who prayed about his own goodness, including his spiritual discipline, and the other who was a tax collector who merely beat his breast and prayed, "God, be merciful to me, a sinner!" (v. 13). Jesus, reflecting on these two men, says that the tax collector "went down to his house justified, rather than the other" (v. 14).

Likewise, in his tirade against the church of Galatia, Paul tells them that they have turned to a different gospel, which is no gospel at all (Gal. 1:6). Why would they do so? He explains what seduced them: "O foolish Galatians! Who has bewitched you? It was before your eyes that Jesus Christ was publicly portrayed as crucified. Let me ask you only this: Did you receive the Spirit by works of the law or by hearing with faith? Are you so foolish? Having begun by the Spirit, are you now being perfected by the flesh?" (3:1–3). The Galatians understood the beginning of the gospel but not its fullness. Their temptation was to accept forgiveness and salvation by grace through faith and then let go of that truth to advance themselves in their flesh rather than by the Spirit.

Too often, Christians replace the messy call of walking in the Spirit and being exposed to the deep things of their heart for a path of goodness that they can achieve in their flesh. This is especially true in the desert and desolation. It is just easier to list a series of spiritual practices to get done than it is to draw near to a holy God. But true spiritual practices are means of grace—they are means of drawing near to God to present yourself to him as he has given himself to you in Jesus.

The Two Tests of Moralism

The Galatians were tempted to do the work only God can do. This is always our temptation. We sometimes assume our only problem is our tendency to do bad things—to explicitly sin—and so our solutions tend to focus on managing our outward behavior. For the moralist, this means seeking our good apart from God or doing the work only God can do in the Christian life. The devastating reality of sin and brokenness reveals how deep the problem goes, that even our spirituality is not pure but is stained by the moralistic impulse to grow through our own resources. Like the Galatians, we are tempted to replace the Spirit by advancing ourselves in the flesh.

What is important to remember is that the Christian life is never *merely* a moral life.[1] It is much more than that. It is a training in holiness, which is first and foremost about God and his presence and secondarily about how we live in the presence of a holy God.[2] When we become Christians, we bring our faith into an already trained character. Our character has been trained in good or bad ways, but before conversion, it was a training in the self and for the self. In other words, our character was trained in the flesh and not in faith; therefore it needs a retraining in faith, hope, and love (see Rom. 14:23).

The training we knew in sin and brokenness was shaped by habits of hiding and covering to manage and manipulate life. This is the training of pride, where we are turned in upon ourselves, seeking to manage and fix our lives in our natural goodness. Many have even learned this natural formation in the church, replacing the training of faith with learning goodness. We all need to consider: How do we discern if we are Christian moralists? How do we live not a mere moral life but a spiritual life?[3]

There are two tests that quickly reveal moralism in the heart: First, when we are convicted by sin, our first and recurring response to guilt is "I'll do better. I'm going to work on that. I'll be better." We are using our own efforts to deal with our badness rather than seeking Christ. This probably leads us to make false promises to God ("God, I promise I'll be better!"). Second, instead of recognizing our failure, sin, and guilt as a path to abide in, depend on, and seek God, we turn to self-rejection by covering rather than uncovering them to the Lord. To abide requires that we come to the Lord in truth and remain in what he has for us. Instead of self-justifying and self-establishing, drawing near to God is trusting that if we remain in him, we will know life abundantly. It is important to pause and consider these two tests a bit more deeply.

The first test is to consider what happens when we are convicted by sin. Being convicted by sin is good; we should be convicted by sin. But anyone with even minor self-awareness can listen to a sermon or read a Scripture passage and realize, *I just heard the ideal of what I should be, but that's not where I am.* If our first and abiding response is to work harder to meet the ideal, then we are moralists. Moralism drives us to turn to our works as the answer for our sin or need instead of turning to Christ.

In the Christian life, contrary to moralism, the first movement is to the cross, to seek Christ in the truth of what he has done for us. That is the answer to our life and struggle. No matter what we experience in life, our call is to continually go to him, trust him, and seek his gracious presence. We go to a God who is not ignorant of our sin, struggle, and brokenness but who has sent his Spirit to groan in our hearts "with groanings too deep for words" (Rom. 8:26).

This test often reveals two lies: first, that we can fix our life and, second, that fixing our life is what God really wants us to do. Instead, our sin and brokenness should lead us to confess, *Lord Jesus, without you I can do nothing* (John 15:5).

But moralism keeps us ignorant of the depths of our sin, making us believe that God simply wants us to perform well. Our temptation is to go to our flesh to try to work out our sin on our own rather than coming out of hiding to seek him. We are tempted to trust ourselves because we find that easier than trusting Christ. This is why the moralist seeks to get out of the desert and desolation at all costs. The goal for the moralist is not seeing their sin and brokenness but just getting past them.

The second test reveals another aspect to this temptation. Instead of seeing one's sin and failure in light of grace, recognizing it as an opportunity to seek God, abide, and know his transforming presence, we shut down because we cannot handle the truth of what our life has become. The truth feels too scary for us because we are still trusting ultimately in ourselves. Instead of recognizing that Christ is our righteousness, we see our lack of righteousness and imagine he is demanding we figure it out on our own. But we need eyes to see the truth; we need faith to remember that we are defined by Christ and his righteousness (see Phil. 3:9). This is why Martin Luther warned, "If Christ is put aside and I look only at myself, then I am done for."[4]

Here is the core dynamic that animates the moralist: *The moralist cannot bear the awareness of being a failure.* The moralist cannot bear the awareness of shame and guilt. The moralist cannot bear to see weakness. This is what they want to get away from. This is the training of the flesh that Adam and Eve immediately brought into creation after the fall. They did not want to experience their shame and guilt, so they immediately responded by covering and hiding rather than attending to it, seeing their helplessness, and looking to God. In a similar sense, we are tempted to read that God's power is made perfect in our weakness (2 Cor. 12:9), underline it in our Bibles, but continue to live and minister in our strength because we cannot bear entering into the truth. But God is the good Father who knows what is best for us and sometimes leads us into the desert and desolation to crack open our hearts to reveal our need for him.

Under the Weight of the Conscience

When I (Kyle) was in college, a missionary organization came to chapel and gave an impassioned talk about helping others, focusing on wealth and poverty, and pointing a harsh finger at our student body. I was overcome with guilt. As a moralist without knowing it, I left with the thought, *I have to be better.* When we walked out of the main chapel into the foyer, there were tables set up with pictures of little kids needing to be sponsored. I looked at those pictures with the experience of guilt fresh in my soul, and I decided to sponsor one of those children.

In listening to the chapel speaker that day, my conscience had panged, telling me that I wasn't what I was supposed to be. There were alarm bells going off in my soul, and I wanted to do something to silence them. When sponsoring a child was presented to me, I accepted that offer, not to serve God, although that's what I thought I was doing. The truth is, I wanted to placate my conscience. I allowed myself to believe I was being faithful, when I was just looking for a way to feel better. It never entered my mind that this was an opportunity to draw near to the Lord in my guilt and shame and in the fear and anxiety I had about him. Instead, I just turned to strategies of my flesh to make those feelings go away.

The problem with the conscience is that we often seek to placate it rather than turning to the Lord. The goal becomes silencing the conscience by doing what we think will make it stop panging. Instead of seeking faithfulness, we want to as-sume that whatever silences our conscience must be faithful. Instead of seeking the Lord, we suppose that the experience of silencing our conscience is a sign of the Lord's accep-tance. Instead of drawing near, we want to believe that our devotion, spiritual practice, or service secures God's favor.

Notice how the conscience turns our attention to our ex-perience of ourselves and then uses that to make us believe we are experiencing God? The conscience doesn't have a perfect link with God's law but is a fallen aspect of our psy-chology. Many Christians, oddly, believe the conscience is the infallible voice of God in their souls. They bear the yoke of their conscience, thinking it is God when they are actually turned in upon themselves, seeking to use their morality to placate the pangs they don't want to experience.

Biblically, the conscience is a psychological response to whatever law has been internalized into your heart.[5] But there are differing kinds of laws you can internalize, based on the life you have lived, the way you were parented, and the way you have come to experience what is good and true. Likewise, Paul argues that the conscience can be misguided, respond-ing to what is false rather than what is true. Importantly, Paul claims that it is in and through our experiences in life that our conscience is formed and transformed, and not simply through information we learn (see 1 Cor. 8:7–12). We do not simply decide what our conscience will respond to, and we cannot transform our broken conscience by shouting the truth into our souls.

Often, however, the conscience will align with God's law. That is both good news and bad. It is good news because it orients us to the truth of God's call, but it is bad news be-cause it also carries with it the law's condemning features. In this latter sense, like the law, the conscience tends to function apart from Christ (see Gal. 3:10–29). The conscience, as William Bridge puts it, understands law but cannot understand Christ's work to satisfy God, which is why it feels like a weight rather than an invitation to know God's grace.[6] We must apply the gospel to our conscience so it leads us to God and not to ourselves.

God gave us a conscience because he wanted us to have a mechanism of the soul that serves as a mirror, showing us when we live against the law we've internalized. This is what the conscience does. It is not meant to be in service of our moralism but in service of our desperate need for Jesus. The conscience should lead us to the cross and not to strategies of the flesh. But in our divided souls, we easily give in to the belief that it is our job to placate our conscience. We come to think that placating the conscience is a sign of faithfulness.

The sad truth is, as I sat in chapel that day, under the accusing weight of my conscience, I sponsored a child because I wanted to feel better and because I wanted to think I had secured God's acceptance. I thought it was my responsibility to deal with the pangs of my conscience because I assumed that was what God wanted. But that was an attempt to take back from Christ the work he had done for me.[7] It was a refusal to embrace his grace. It was a rejection of the way of Christ to try to generate a way of life from within my goodness.

Dietrich Bonhoeffer was particularly attuned to this problem with the conscience, claiming that our "conscience pretends to be the voice of God."[8] Rather than being the actual voice of God, the conscience masquerades as a new standard for the soul to live up to in order to justify itself. It aims to be a law that we can use as a mirror to decide if we are being faithful enough. As with the law, we often use it moralistically to avoid drawing near to God himself. Bonhoeffer continues, revealing the nefarious depths the conscience can employ: "Indeed it is the function of the conscience to make human beings flee from God. . . . Conscience chases humankind away from God into its secure hiding place. Here, far away from God, humankind itself plays the role of being judge and in this way seeks to evade God's judgment. . . . Conscience is not the voice of God within sinful human beings; instead it is precisely their defense against this voice."[9]

The conscience, meant to lead us to God, becomes the strategy to avoid him, manage him, or secure ourselves without really repenting. Notice how subtle and deceptive the flesh and moralism can be. This is why the Protestant tradition, especially the evangelical tradition, has always been a "filthy rags" tradition. We always knew that our greatest temptation as Christians was not abandoning the faith but using the things of God to hide from him—using the "filthy rags" of our works to imagine we can placate an angry deity. The true path of the conscience should be to God and not to ourselves because a life lived in and through the self can only be a life of death. This is why the desert and desolation are gifts; it is in those places that we learn that God is our all in all.

Importantly, the conscience, like the law, is not the problem (see Rom. 7:13). The problem is our tendency to take what God gives us and use it according to the flesh and not the Spirit. This is especially true with our devotion, as Jesus makes clear in his critique of the religious leadership. The problem is that we can feel a pang of conscience, as I did in that college chapel, moralistically silence our conscience, and believe we've secured God's praise. We imagine God is placated, in other words, and that his anger has abated. We have, in Bonhoeffer's words, escaped God's judgment because we have created a judge we can manage and manipulate. We avoid God and then tell ourselves that this avoidance is faithfulness.

Our Moralistic Defense

When Paul describes the conscience, he claims that when the conscience pangs, the accusing and excusing thoughts emerge from the heart (see Rom. 2:15). These thoughts are the strategies of a fallen self to defend against the condemning nature of the conscience. Under the weight of the experience of condemnation, we turn to strategies to feel better instead of turning to the one place help can truly be found. This is why moralism and the conscience always go hand in hand. The moralist wants to avoid the messy truth at all costs; moral effort, ministry, and devotion are often the easiest ways to do that.

It is significant that our strategies move in opposing directions, one self-accusation and the other self-defense. The accusing thoughts are often used to try to generate faithfulness by using guilt and shame to pump up our will: *Why don't you get your act together? What is wrong with you?!* Or, in contrast, the defending thoughts try to deflect the experience of condemnation: *It could be worse. You're better than you used to be. At least you're not as bad as that friend of yours.* Both strategies stem from deep beliefs that we can manage our sin in our goodness, and so instead of seeing the truth, we self-condemn or self-justify. In contrast, the conscience should lead us to Christ. In the strategies of the flesh, we try to fix what only the blood of Christ can purify (see Heb. 9:14).

Moralistically responding to our conscience is fleshly in all seasons of life, but it is in the desert and desolation that we really see how broken and sinful this is. In these seasons, we feel overwhelmed by our sinful autonomy because we are experiencing how much we are still trying to self-save, self-secure, and use our self-righteousness to sustain us. We see the truth, and without consolation upholding us, we become overwhelmed by how much we need to change and how broken we really are. This can feel debilitating. But the invitation in this is to lay down the old strategies of the flesh and the old map of moralism and draw near to Christ in our brokenness, confusion, and sinfulness.

What becomes difficult for some is that the conscience can be "seared" (1 Tim. 4:2). Sometimes a seared conscience does not pang at all, and a person loses the sense of living in rebellion. The person becomes numb to their sin. At other times, however, a seared conscience is one that has been frozen in an accusatory or defensive state. A seared accusatory conscience is debilitating, keeping a person under a self-imposed wrath they assume is from God. This often leads a person to moralistically silence this unappeasable voice, living a kind of despairing life and never feeling release.

A seared defensive conscience, on the other hand, causes a person to avoid the truth of what they have become in the flesh. Often, this goes hand in hand with a view of God where God no longer cares much about our sin or his grace is no longer connected to the call for obedience. Both accusatory and defensive strategies undermine God's grace and calling. Both avoid God in a quest to navigate condemnation on their own. Neither offers freedom because neither truly leads to Christ.

As should be clear, the problem of moralism and the experience of our conscience are intertwined. They both take things that are good and true—we should be good, and we should have a clear conscience—and turn them into ways to live in the flesh. For both, the initial problem comes with how we experience our failure and how we relate to ourselves in it. Often, it is only by attending to our self-talk that we can see how we really understand the conscience. If our immediate inclination is that God wants us to ignore the truth of our lives or that God cannot handle the truth, this reveals we are already functioning moralistically apart from the gospel. In this, we have become like the Galatians, beginning in the Spirit, but now trying to perfect ourselves in the flesh (Gal. 3:3). Instead, it is time to come out of hiding to draw near to Christ and seek him in the truth.

Retraining the Conscience

When the moralist's conscience pangs, they think, *I need to be better. I should be better. I have to figure out ways to be better.* Being better is the goal, which reveals our fleshly solution to the pangs of the conscience. This is the old habit of seeing consolation as the answer. So instead of going to the Lord, the moralist turns to themselves and their own moral resources. The moralist is looking for a way to stop the conscience from panging—to make the feelings of guilt and shame go away—that is the point. The moralist is a person who still thinks they can advance themselves in their flesh to fulfill the law. The law and the conscience, in this sense, are intertwined realities.

By faith, the pangs of our conscience, like the law, are meant to lead us to Christ and not to ourselves (see Gal. 3:24). The author of Hebrews tells us that only the blood of Christ can cleanse the conscience, and it cleanses it from "dead works" (9:14). These dead works are the works we use to silence the conscience in our own efforts instead of coming to Jesus. These are the dead works of moralism. Confronted with the ideal of the Christian life in Scripture or through a sermon, the Christian must reject the claims of the flesh and draw near to God through the blood of Jesus. Under the weight of our sin and brokenness we need to take the yoke of Jesus, a yoke that is easy and light (Matt. 11:29–30). We trust in Christ and wait upon the consolation he may give and not the consolation we can generate on our own.

In retraining our conscience in the truth, we must be willing to see our life for what it is. Our conscience will still pang when we hear a sermon or see the ideal Christian existence depicted. But instead of looking for ways to placate an angry conscience—looking for a god we can appease in our goodness—we must turn to the truth:

> *Lord, look at this. The first thing my heart turns to are strategies to manage and manipulate you rather than be with you. Father, I need you here. I need you in these places of my heart that want to be good rather than be with you. I need you to meet me in the places where I want to abide in myself rather than abiding in you. I need you in all the ways that I want to bear fruit of myself rather than bearing your fruit. Lord, have mercy.*

Retraining the conscience requires that I reorder it from myself to God, such that its panging leads me to God to abide in him in light of what is true of me.

The conscience is meant to lead me to Christ in my neediness, failures, and sin. This will be a struggle. Often, our conscience will pang and our flesh will offer up scripts to try to manage and manipulate God.

❖ *God, I am so sorry; I won't do it again.*
❖ *God, I'll be better.*

❖ *God, I'll do whatever it takes; just give me another chance.*

If you pay attention to your soul, you'll see that your heart isn't even in these prayers. You say them precisely to avoid entering into them. These scripts are a kind of smoke screen to keep God at bay. Adam said, "Run! Hide!" while we pray, "God, I'll be better." There is often no difference between them. This is why the self gets exhausted in the desert and desolation.

Projects of the Moral Self

No amount of effort, no amount of spiritual discipline, no amount of work can ever fix you or deal with your shame and guilt. If that were the case, then the Christian life would simply be a moral life. But that is not the Christian life. The Christian life is not fundamentally about being good. It is not ultimately about obedience to a set of principles we hear from a preacher. It is not even solely about trying to imitate Jesus, as if Jesus took on flesh, lived in faithfulness, and died for our sins just to show us a pattern of life that could be lived apart from him. All these things can still be projects of the self in the flesh, even if they are the projects of a moral self in the flesh.

In seeing how the flesh uses the conscience moralistically, we can see the lie that made Paul so furious with the Galatians. The lie tells us that sin is just a list of bad things we do, and so we learn the list so we can stop doing bad things. Rather, in Scripture, the lie of the flesh is that you can live a life for God from yourself and your own resources. This is what it means to begin in the Spirit and continue in the flesh (Gal. 3:3). This is what Paul tells the Colossians is "self-made religion," which has the "appearance of wisdom" but is fueled by spiritual discipline that has no ability to deal with the true problems of our sinful condition (Col. 2:23). Trying to advance themselves in the flesh, the Colossians sought to grow in autonomy. Perhaps the greatest temptation in the Christian life is to grow oneself. This is what we continually fail to recognize.

New Testament scholar Grant Macaskill helps to reveal how devastating moralism truly is. He claims that when many evangelical churches talk about growth, they do so in a way that is "often functionally Christless."[10] He explains,

> The way we *actually* think about the moral activity or growth of the Christian (what we often label "discipleship") is not really Christ-centered: we can talk about being "Christlike" or about "relying on the power of the Spirit" but still think about this as something *we* do. When, with the Holy Spirit's help, we are obedient, we are simply better versions of ourselves.[11]

Some of us may be wondering, *What is the problem here?* The idea that we are to be "better versions of ourselves" seems obvious. Yet what we find in Scripture is something more profound. Our only hope, Macaskill explains, is for a better self to inhabit our lives.[12] So, Paul says, "It is no longer I who live, but Christ who lives in me" (Gal. 2:20). Our hope is Christ and Christ alone.

The Christian life, at some point, will require us to wake up and finally realize, *God, this isn't working. My morality isn't working. My own agenda isn't giving me rivers of living water. My obedience isn't establishing the life of love I so desperately want.* What few realize but all must come to grapple with is that to mature in the faith, we need to see that we are not the ones making this work. When we finally hit that point, we are ready to see that the spiritual life requires denouncing the moral life of the flesh.

The spiritual life requires us to reject all ways we try to find happiness by dealing with our shame and guilt in our own power. The difficult truth of following Jesus is that we must lose our lives to find them. Similarly, we have to lose our moral self-help projects to embrace a supernaturally holy life. This opens us to a new kind of consolation in the love of Jesus, not a consolation we generate to avoid the desert or desolation, and not even the early consolation we once had. This new consolation is one that has been shaped by the desert and desolation—it is the solid food of adult joy and peace that the Lord provides in his love.

EXPERIENCE

Both our conscience and our goodness can blind us to the reality of our lives. Sometimes we need to be confronted with a harsh mirror in order to see the truth. We see this happen in 2 Samuel 12, where Nathan goes to David and tells him a parable about a rich man and a poor man and how the rich man stole the poor man's precious lamb because he couldn't be bothered to take one from his own flock. The parable awakens deep anger in David, who is ready to kill the rich man, until Nathan reveals that the parable is about David himself, who took Uriah's wife, Bathsheba, and then had him killed to cover it up. Now, confronted with the truth, David's conscience is awakened, leaving him with the dread of judgment upon him.

David recognizes that the Lord wants "truth in the inward being" and "wisdom in the secret heart" (Ps. 51:6). He recognizes that his panging conscience should awaken him to the truth and lead him to the only place to know forgiveness, grace, and mercy—the Lord.

Pray David's prayer from Psalm 51 as a way to draw near and offer your life to the Lord, and open your heart and your conscience to him:

❖ *Lord, what do I do when I feel my conscience pang? Do I turn to you? Do I look for ways to be good so that I don't feel my conscience any longer?*

❖ *Lord, when the accusing and defending thoughts arise in my heart, which do I tend to turn to? Do I accuse myself, thinking that doing so will appease you? Do I defend myself, looking for ways to justify my actions?*

❖ *Lord, what would it look like to bring all this to you? Lord, show me what I should bring you. Show me how to tell you the truth of what is going on in my soul and let you clean me and sanctify me thoroughly by your forgiveness, presence, and love.*

7

Avoiding God in Our Devotion

When I (John) was wandering in the desert, I remember trying to bolster my weak and dry prayer life by trying to infuse energy and devotion into my time with the Lord. I would pause and give myself pep talks about loving God more, being more faithful, and seeking him more diligently. Rather than seeing the truth and coming out of hiding from God, I tried to take my spiritual life into my own hands. Unfortunately, at the time, I had no way of seeing this.

In a similar way, when I (Kyle) was walking through a season of the desert, I remember trying to use the fruit I was seeing in my ministry to uphold me. Instead of turning my eyes to Jesus and trusting that he is my life, my strength, and my all, I was trying to secure myself using worldly metrics of success. Our devotion to God is good, but like all good things God gives us, we are tempted to use it to secure ourselves rather than seeking and trusting in him. We are tempted to turn our devotional lives into places to make life feel more meaningful rather than laying down our lives to him. Our devotion is particularly susceptible to the flesh because we assume it is the one place our action is pure.

Jesus calls us to walk with him in such a way that we allow him to define us and secure our identity, value, and goodness. It is only in losing our lives that we find them in him. But our temptation is to think this is true of our initial salvation but that we now must move beyond this. We are tempted to think we are saved at the cross and then formed through our own savvy and effort. But spiritual formation is not actualizing ourselves. Spiritual formation is losing our self-made and self-established life to know life in Christ. Put differently, to embrace the way of Jesus requires that we accept that Christianity is not primarily about our transformation but is first and foremost about life through death—losing our life to find life in Christ and the Spirit.

Rather than tweaking our activities, or pumping up our wills, Jesus speaks a more profound truth: "Whoever would save his life will lose it, but whoever loses his life for my sake will find it" (Matt. 16:25). Paul similarly writes, "I have been crucified with Christ. It is no longer I who live, but Christ who lives in me. And the life I now live in the flesh I live by faith in the Son of God, who loved me and gave himself for me" (Gal. 2:20). Our faith involves death and resurrection and not simply a boost to get the life we want. This is why our spiritual discipline is talked about in terms of putting off the old man and putting on the new (Eph. 4:20–24). We have died with Christ, and so we must consider ourselves "dead to sin and alive to God in Christ Jesus" (Rom. 6:11). In this new existence of life in Christ, we discover that we journey with the purifying fire who calls forth the deep things of the heart to transform them in and through his love.

Sin in the Depths

To walk with the purifying fire is to accept that in his presence the truth of our heart leaks out. This is what purifying fires do. Being with God causes impurities to emerge because, as the purifying fire of love, God always awakens the truth. Unfortunately, as we have seen, we often assume the opposite. We assume God's presence only awakens joy and our goodness, concealing our sins rather than exposing them. We end up affirming that God is the purifying fire without attending to what that will mean in our experience.

The problem is even worse when we assume that our devotional acts are pure and unadulterated. We assume acts of devotion are pristine realities of our lives that we simply need to inflate to drown out our sinful actions. But it turns out that it is easy to declare, "Of all the sinners, I am the worst" (see 1 Tim. 1:15) because it feels like the right thing to say. But we can do so without attending to the truth of our sin. Even our devotion, service, and worship are veined with vice in various ways, and the Lord leaves nothing untouched in his desire to purify and transform.

Sin and brokenness run much deeper than we are often aware. The Lord wants to show us that where sin abounds, grace abounds all the more (Rom. 5:20). But that path requires that we see how much sin really does abound in us, even in our good works. In showing these things to us, the Lord wants us to learn, in the deepest way, that Christ is our life, Christ is our righteousness, and Christ is even our sanctification (see 1 Cor. 1:30). He is weaning us off ourselves and onto him so that we can only ever boast in him (see Eph. 2:8–10). This is the way of love that moves us from knowing love only in our exuberant youthfulness to being seen and known by Christ in the truth and coming to know his mercy, forgiveness, and love where we most need it.

The Truth We Don't Want to See

When God led us into the desert and early consolation faded, he showed us what was in our hearts. We were confronted with pride, envy, greed, lust, and grandiosity. We saw ways we had been trying to use God to get life on our own terms. We saw how idolatry had made its way not only into our hearts but into our faith. But through this we began to see how being with God in these things, seeking him and abiding in him, had led to a deeper and more profound rest in his presence. As with all our relationships, we can fear that difficult truths might destroy the relationship, but it is often revealing the truth that becomes the catalyst for growth. So too in our life with the Lord.

After journeying through the desert, many come to know a deeper form of consolation than before. It is different from early consolation. Consolation has grown with us. As our desires transform from our childhood to our adulthood, so too consolation develops and deepens in our maturation. No longer grounded in our passion but with more deeply fueled affection, we can see what the Lord was doing in the desert, and this helps to fund a more abiding praise. What was immature pleasure in youth can become joy, gratitude, and love as we mature.

But this new season of consolation awakens another temptation. Now we are tempted to think we have deciphered the hidden formula of the Christian life. *Finally,* we think, *we are out of the desert! Finally, we're back in consolation. Now we have to make sure we don't lose it again!* We think we've learned what we need to know to walk with the Lord deeply, but then a second darkness emerges. This is something more disorienting than just losing consolation. We discover the experience of being lost and abandoned.

Throughout the Christian tradition, we have used many words to describe this experience. Sometimes it is called the dark night of the soul, desolation, or spiritual desertion. In this darkness the Lord is illumining something new. There will no doubt be some features of sin that arise quickly. But the goal of this second darkness is to expose not explicit sin but the fleshliness of our goodness. Before the purifying fire of the Lord, we come to see that even our devotion has been warped in sin and brokenness.

The experience of abandonment, which is how this is often described, reveals a person's deep character. What makes this even more confusing, as Puritan theologian William Perkins notes, is that sometimes God removes his Spirit's assistance from us so that we are "left to fall into some actual and grievous sin."[1] God's action in our lives actually awakens sin, not because God is causing us to sin but because he stops upholding us in pleasure to reveal the truth of our character and devotion. He is revealing to us what we would be without his continual assistance. This is to unearth spiritual pride.

God withdraws his consolation because spiritual pride is so easily hidden and because we often try to use pride to root out other sins in our lives. Think about that. We use spiritual pride as leverage to deal with our sin, puffing ourselves up with how good we are becoming as Christians! Secretly, we begin to believe that our action is securing our growth. The Lord removes his assistance so that people are fully confronted with their hidden sins in order to lead the person into humility.[2] In this state, what Protestants often call "spiritual desertion," the Christian cannot recognize the difference between themselves and those cast away from God.[3] But, Perkins explains, the Lord does not truly desert his children. In this season, the Lord is calling us to draw near to him and trust in him by faith. Through this desertion, the Lord is cultivating humility in our lives and unearthing our depths so that we can know his love in our brokenness, pain, and sorrow.

Exposed to a Deeper Truth

Unlike the desert, where everything seems flat, desolation feels more disorienting. One of the reasons for this disorientation is that we are used to seeing sin as an aspect of ourselves that we want to leave behind, while subconsciously we hold on to our virtues and think, *Well, at least I have these.* This is what is being most directly addressed in this season.[4] The gift of the Lord is that he is showing you how your virtue, obedience, and devotion are still mired in the flesh. In this season, God is moving you away not only from a *sensual* Christianity—where you are using your senses to measure God's presence and your goodness—but even from your virtues and spiritual efforts as a way to secure yourself. The Lord is shepherding you to live by faith to trust in him and his righteousness alone (see Phil. 3:9).

The call to live by faith is difficult because we are trained in our flesh to live by sight. To live by sight is to live according to our senses rather than according to how God has revealed the kingdom in and through his Word (see 2 Cor. 5:7). In the season of desolation, we discover how much of our Christian devotion and obedience are fueled not by faith but by sight, not by God's grace but by our virtuous efforts in the flesh. We come to see that we have internalized equations in our souls that we use to determine if we are doing well. What the Lord is revealing is that we are using the sight of flesh as a mirror to see our goodness. We want to gaze at ourselves and our formation instead of looking to Jesus.

The way this works out, for some, is that they recognize their Bible reading has become a way to avoid God. It feels good to read a chapter of the Bible at the beginning of the day. It feels like they are progressing. But when that feeling disappears and it all feels dead, then they are being shown what is really fueling their devotion. The question is where this experience leads them: Will this deadness cause them to draw near to the Lord by faith, or will they go looking for other avenues to live by their senses to reawaken their passion so they feel better? For many, praise seems to uphold and fuel their love of the Lord, but in desolation, they feel like everything is lost. When this happens, where do we turn? Do we turn to passion or to Christ? We often try to pump up our wills—exciting ourselves with passion—to try to feel alive again instead of drawing near to the Lord in the truth of what is going on in our souls.

In this season, we experience sadness in relation to our spiritual practices because the Lord is showing us how much of our devotion is being fueled by the flesh. What emerges is that selfishness, grandiosity, and the desire for pleasure were sustaining our spiritual practices. We might discover that we serve in the church because we want to be perceived in a certain way. Maybe we continue to give because we imagine it will prod God to make our lives work the way we want. Or we begin to realize that our Christian actions and practices are attempts to manage our feelings of guilt, shame, fear, and anxiety. There is a massive difference between using God to fix your life and knowing that Christ is your life (Col. 3:4). This is what this second darkness invites you more deeply into.

It is important to pause, consider our developmental maturation in love, and ask ourselves these questions:

❖ *Am I open to seeing the truth of my life, or has my Christian life been constructed around the deep desire to avoid seeing the truth?*

❖ *What would need to happen for me to see the truth of how deep sin, pain, and rebellion have really gone in my life? Would I choose to attend to these things in consolation if I weren't forced to? Would I choose to navigate the hidden pride and spiritual arrogance in my soul if the Lord didn't illumine it?*

❖ *What would it take for me to be open to seeing that I am more interested in using God to secure the life I want than laying down my life and accepting the life he has for me?*

The desert and desolation are not what we want, but they are the realities we need to mature. Avoiding them, or looking to get out of them, is like trying to avoid the demands of adulthood.

The Gift of Desolation

To walk the path of Christian maturation, we need to see the ways we try to fix ourselves through our devotion, service, and obedience rather than using them as ways to "present [our] bodies as a living sacrifice" (Rom. 12:1). Put differently, we need to see if we are using God as a form of self-help. Instead of self-help, God transforms our souls in and through love and shepherds us into places of love so that we can overflow with love. What we discover in this is that the Spirit is not purifying us away from our longing for joy, happiness, and spiritual pleasure. God wants us to long for those things. But he wants us to long for those things because we long for him.

In this season, God is showing us the ways we long for things that help us feel devoted *over* longing for him. The gift in this season is to see the truth so that we can embrace God in the truth. The curse of this season is thinking that our calling is to fix our spiritual lives in our own power or that God is pushing us back on our own resources. Instead, we need to know that it was in our sin that Christ died for us and that he calls us to himself even in these places. He wants us to know, in our depths, that without him we can do nothing (John 15:5). The truth is that the Lord wants to reveal to us, more and more, how deep his grace really goes. He wants to show us that we accept his grace in part when he wants us to have the whole.

It never dawned on us early in our Christian lives that we could admit the truth to the Lord, that he would want us to be with him in our sin, brokenness, and struggle, and that realizing this was a gift. Like Paul, who comes to boast in his weaknesses as well as in things like insults, calamities, and persecutions, we can now see how our weakness, brokenness, and sin are opportunities to grasp Christ (see 2 Cor. 12:9–10). This is the path of humility because this is the path of losing our lives for Christ to find them in him.

In following Jesus, we are called to learn not only that we are saved by grace but also that we only grow by grace. It is easier to turn our devotion into ways to be good, or ways to tether God to ourselves, than it is to receive his grace and offer ourselves to him. It is hard for the moralist to see and believe this. Growing up in the faith is, in part, coming to see how we can grow with and in him only by his grace.

The gift of desolation will make us confront the ways we are not interested in this kind of growth. Desolation reveals how much of our devotion and life are given to fleshly forms of growth. We should never assume we are beyond being tempted by growing ourselves in the flesh as opposed to the Spirit (see Gal. 3:1–3).

Finding Love in the Deep Places

For many, seasons of desolation come upon them unexpectedly. It may even take a while to notice. Many folks only come to know they are in a season of desolation when they begin despairing about what they do *for God*. Think of the older brother in Jesus's parable who doesn't rejoice in the life he has received from his father but instead complains, "Look, these many years I have served you" (Luke 15:29). He has come to see himself as a servant rather than as a son of his father. In similar ways, in this season, the very actions that seemed to be funded by our gratitude now feel dead. We begin to wonder if any of them have been making a difference. We might even admit to ourselves, *I don't even know why I do any of this*. With the psalmist, we might begin to wonder, *Has all of this been done in vain?* (see Psalm 73:13).

In consolation, our own devotion and service felt deep and rich and filled with gratitude. No doubt much of our experience and gratitude to God were genuine and true of us. But there were also fleshly things that consolation hid from sight. In desolation, those fleshly things come to the fore, and we are in danger of losing sight of how genuine our faith has been. Importantly, there is real faith, hope, and love in the heart of a Christian, even though they may be hard to find in desolation.[5] There is a real love of God in your deep places, but what desolation first reveals is that it has

127

not fully invaded your character. This season will shepherd you into loving God in your character by first showing you what your character has become. But this does not feel like a gift. This feels like everything has been in vain.

It is important to remember, however, that desolation is often necessary because we struggle to see how vice-laden our virtue is when we are in consolation. Our goodness is still good in a very real sense. But even our goodness needs purification from sin and self because the opposite of sin is not simply goodness but faith (see Rom. 14:23). This requires a shift from trusting in ourselves and our flesh to trusting in Christ. In our youth, we couldn't see this. In our youth, badness was simply a list of sins that we needed to stop desiring and being seduced by, and goodness was the opposite.

In our adulthood, what we will be tempted by more than anything is to ignore the hidden and deceptive sins of our goodness, especially in places of devotion, virtue, or ministry. For some, the Lord will reveal how much jealousy fuels their ministry. Others might be shown how a form of greed actually fuels their giving or how grandiosity and selfish ambition fuel their service. We've met many pastors who have tapped into anger rather than love to animate their ministry but who are unable to see it until everything comes crashing down.

One of the first assignments I (Kyle) give my seminary students is an hour-long prayer project in which they draw near to the Lord to present their lives to him. I have them ask the Lord, "Lord, why did I come to seminary? What am I doing here? What do you have for me in this season?" I have my students do this as a way to be "watchful" in prayer, as Paul calls us to (Col. 4:2). I ask them to be watchful to see what their hearts do in the presence of the Lord because when we draw near to God, our hearts reveal our treasures.

I'll never forget what one student said to me after this assignment. He pulled me aside after the next class and said, "Professor, I wanted to tell you in person that I'm dropping out of seminary. As I was offering this to the Lord, I was finally able to admit the truth, which I think I already knew but wasn't being honest about. I'm at seminary because I like to be seen as right, and I want to win arguments. I'm here because of my grandiosity. I even knew it wasn't good for my marriage, that it was going to hurt my marriage, and I didn't care. I hope I'm back one day, but I need to devote myself to other things right now."

Praise God that this student could see that even going to seminary might be mired in the flesh! Seminary education is a wonderful thing, but just like everything else, it can be a seedbed for the flesh.

Do Not Grow Weary

In desolation, confronted with fleshliness even in our devotion, we will be tempted to grow fainthearted. Paul, for instance, knew that the Christian life would cause us to grow weary in doing good, and so he encourages us by reminding us that if we continue with the Lord, we will bear fruit (see Gal. 6:9). The author of Hebrews, likewise, encourages us to look to Jesus as our example so we "may not grow weary or fainthearted" (Heb. 12:3), reminding us that God "disciplines us for our good, that we may share his holiness. For the moment all discipline seems painful rather than pleasant, but later it yields the peaceful fruit of righteousness to those who have been trained by it" (vv. 10–11).

It is easier to memorize verses about not growing weary than it is to not grow weary when we are overcome with weariness. In desolation specifically, we will be tempted by thinking, *None of this is working.* Seeing how fleshly even our devotion and service have become can leave our actions feeling flat and pointless. Confronted with this experience, we are again tempted to either abandon our activities or try to reinvigorate them with passion. Many sadly just accept dullness as the new normal and give up on a deeper journey with the Lord. This latter option is accepted by many who are hardworking, diligent, and often heavily involved in ministry. But this experience is an invitation from God to recognize that something is wrong and that we need to turn to him regardless of what is going on.

The place we often hear this invitation, even if we are not yet able to hear it, is in our spiritual practice. In consolation, spiritual practices are life-giving. They are places overflowing with rejoicing and gratitude. In the desert, our spiritual practices begin to feel fatiguing. In desolation, spiritual practices feel bad because the Lord is using them to mirror our soul back to us, showing us what is in our heart.

The difficulty we find in desolation is that we are still called to offer our lives to the Lord in all things, but now all those things mirror back our vice, brokenness, and struggle. Going to church is no longer joyful, but we experience angst, anger, or maybe just sadness. Reading the Bible leads us into feelings of desperation and even condemnation because we see how much of our life with the Lord has been fueled by the flesh.

Once again, desolation is an opportunity to seek Christ in the truth and to know his righteousness instead of our own (see Phil. 3:1–10). But many are tempted to despair under the weight of their sin and brokenness instead of turning to Christ. Many are drowning beneath the seas of condemnation, still seeking to use their own goodness or devotion to buoy their life before God.

In these seasons, folks long for spiritual practices to provide reprieve and to be a life vest of hope when they are thrashing against the waves, but instead these practices feel like weights that drag them down into the darkness. Spiritual practices mirror back brokenness and sin in the desert and desolation, and we often interpret this as failure and experience it as heavy and fatiguing. What this means is that these practices now reveal our insides—our lack of love, our boredom, or something like loneliness—instead of providing experiences of consolation. When spiritual practices become mirrors, it is tempting to go looking for other practices that might bring back consolation or quiet our guilt and shame. Too many, despairing of their former joy, wonder if they are lost and if God has left them alone.

In seasons of desolation, our call is to wait upon the Lord. We wait upon him by refusing to use devotion or service to fix our lives or to try to get out of the desert or desolation. We are not called to change our experiences; we are called to present ourselves to the Lord (Rom. 6:13). As we do so, offering ourselves to him in the truth, we must accept that this path will be one where he unravels the false structures we've been using as crutches. He is eroding the ways we've been fueling our Christian lives with the flesh.

Desolation is a cure for a self-fueled spirituality. The Lord is taking away our deep belief that we know the right formula to make the Christian life work. Desolation always calls us to the Lord in our weakness and brokenness for dependence on him, where he reveals that his power is made perfect in our weakness (2 Cor. 12:9). Desolation takes us from merely affirming that Christ is the only answer for our sin and brokenness to actually living this out in our deepest needs and desires.

In early consolation—and to a lesser extent, the desert—we carry the burden of the flesh, but we don't feel it. We only feel the burden fully in desolation. Until then, our flesh doesn't feel as weighty because we're considering it through the lens of our virtues and our intention to be faithful. We don't experience its weight because we assume our goodness, devotion, and service are pure. But the Lord reveals the truth to purify these with his love, in his love, for the sake of love. He is showing us not only that our initial salvation is by grace alone but that the entirety of the Christian life is by grace.

Beyond Leveling Up

There are always two paths presented to us: One is a moral path that seeks to create a life in our own power through goodness, devotion, service, and such, and the other is a spiritual path that increasingly abides in and depends on the Lord because we recognize more and more how desperately we need him. The first path can create a good citizen and a nice church member, but it won't be the formation of someone humble and lowly, filled with the Spirit, and overflowing in grace. Only the second path is one of humility—true humility—where our hope does not reside within ourselves and our own resources but in God.

On the first path, we think of human formation as leveling up, modifying, or maximizing our resources. This kind of growth is focused on adjusting our activities but is not focused on becoming the *kind of person we need to be to live in the presence of God*. Natural formation is taking who we are and merely advancing ourselves. But spiritual formation is never simply tacking on upgrades to an already decent person; it is first and foremost about death and resurrection. In consolation, this is exciting. But in the desert and desolation, it feels painful. Biblical spirituality requires that we lose our life to find it and that we continually put

132

off the old and put on the new, trusting less in the flesh and more in God. Whether in consolation or in desolation, our call is to follow him and trust him on this journey of love.

It is easy to believe that our growth is a simple development rather than a continual dying and rising. We can seclude death and resurrection to our conversion and fail to see that Scripture depicts the whole of our life with God as a continual death and resurrection. In desolation, we are called to lay down our lives to find them in Christ as we see more and more of the things we still hold on to. Through desolation, we can now say with more depth of knowledge, *Lord, I believe; help me in all of this unbelief* (see Mark 9:24). Through desolation we bring our life to the Lord and present ourselves to him, saying, *Lord, look at the desires of my heart. Look at what I long for. Lord, I want you. I want to long for these things only in you and with you. I don't want to just try to achieve, succeed, or survive on my own and through my own abilities. I want to be with you. I don't want to merely be good, I want to bear the fruit of the Spirit as I abide in Christ.*

EXPERIENCE

Consider your life with the Lord, and attend to all the practices you have given yourself to: going to church, participating in small groups, missions, serving, hosting, studying, praying, worshiping, evangelizing, and so on. Ask the Lord:

❖ *Lord, when I have grown tired or when these activities haven't gone as I expected, who have I turned to?*

Have I turned to you, or have I turned to myself and tried to figure out what to do better?

❖ *Lord, when I have struggled to care about what you care about, have I sought to generate passion or devotion in my own power to get excited about these things, masking the truth of my heart, or have I been able to honestly come to you?*

❖ *In these hard times, have I just pressed on in resignation and not been open to what my struggles were telling me about the state of my soul?* [Share with the Lord what the desert and desolation have been for you.]

❖ *Have I struggled with envy, looking at other people worshiping, serving, or just thriving, and coveted their flourishing? Have I sought to generate the life I want, or have I sought you, Lord?*

Pray the words of Psalm 73 and be open to the ways you, like the psalmist, have grown envious of others (like the wicked) and maybe even despaired of your devotion. Feel his angst when he prays, "All in vain have I kept my heart clean and washed my hands in innocence" (v. 13). But notice as well how the psalm shifts. The psalmist says that he struggled to understand how he should think about these things, and so he took them into the presence of the Lord (v. 17). Only in the Lord's sanctuary did he begin to have eyes to see the truth and recognize that the Lord's work is deeper than he imagined. Bring your life to the Lord and present the truth to him, not just generally but the truth of how you have tried to use your devotion, goodness, and commitment to tether him to yourself to get your life the way you want it. Be open to your need of him and tell him exactly all you feel and all you need.

8

Avoiding God
by Fixing Ourselves

I (Kyle) remember a moment of my life when I began despairing. *Will I ever grow beyond these struggles? Will I ever get beyond this temptation?* I was fatigued because, without realizing it, I had been trying to fix my life in my own power, and my spiritual life began to feel heavy. Suddenly the things that were so life-giving started feeling like a burden. Seeing the Bible sitting on my table no longer felt like an invitation but simply woke guilt in my soul. Hearing sermons did not unearth possibility in me but made me feel like growth was impossible, and guilt, shame, fear, and anxiety became ever-present realities. I started to despair because I had lost grip on the truth of the gospel, and so I forgot that these were opportunities to grasp Christ and not just fix myself.

In these seasons, I remember countless times when I left a church service, chapel, or Bible study with the feeling, *I've got to get my act together*. On some occasions I was confronted with a particular sin that I kept falling back into. Other times it was just the sense that I wasn't as zealous as I should be. Sometimes it was a Bible passage that just struck me:

- ❖ "Pray without ceasing" (1 Thess. 5:17).
- ❖ "Do not be anxious about anything" (Phil. 4:6).
- ❖ "Be holy, for I am holy" (1 Pet. 1:16).
- ❖ "Be filled with the Spirit" (Eph. 5:18).

When I was confronted with these truths in the earliest years of my faith, I would just say, "Yes! That is right. Let's go!" But as time went on, these passages woke something deeper in me. Instead of being captivated by God's goodness and grace, I felt his judgment and my failure. Instead of being excited about the possibility of obedience, I felt the impossibility of my faithfulness.

Rediscovering the Heart of Spiritual Formation

When consolation fades and we feel stuck in the Christian life, the temptation is to try to pump up our will, excite passion, and fuel our faithfulness through our flesh. But over time, we begin to feel the effects of trying to live off an overly caffeinated will. Or, instead of infusing passion into our will, we might focus on getting the right technique or affirming the right doctrinal statement, assuming that this will secure the solution we want. The assumption is that we simply need to tweak our actions to get the right results.

We have seen, with the church at Galatia, that we will always be tempted to begin with the Spirit but try to advance ourselves in the flesh (Gal. 3:3). Rather than drawing near to Christ in our neediness, we are tempted to create a path where God becomes an instrument we use for our own advancement. Even more troubling is that early consolation leads us to believe that we have basically figured out life, so we just need to understand more, serve more, and worship more, and things will keep on getting better. When the desert hits, things get confusing. When desolation hits, we tend to discover a deep and abiding anger we never knew was in our hearts. Sometimes, left without consolation, people just begin to despair.

The temptation of the flesh, like Satan's temptation in the garden, promises much but delivers nothing that lasts. Like Satan's lies, the flesh promises a path to being like God through our own efforts and action, but it proves fruitless. This is what Paul calls "self-made religion" that has "no value in stopping the indulgence of the flesh" (Col. 2:23). This way appears wise, Paul tells us, but fails because it seeks to make Jesus and his way into a bulleted list of ways to grow. *Jesus himself* is our salvation, our hope, our righteousness, and our sanctification (see 1 Cor. 1:30). This leads us to a truth that is incredibly easy to miss: Our spiritual growth and formation are not primarily about our growth or our formation.

Spiritual formation is about God—who he is and what he has done for us—and about how, in Christ Jesus, by his Spirit, we can know life, holiness, and righteousness. Spiritual formation is about putting our faith and hope in God, loving him with our whole heart, and loving our neighbor as ourself. We are formed in his life, by his life, for life with him as we are filled with his Spirit. But our formation is not the goal. Our formation is the fruit of the union we have with God in Christ. He is the goal. The whole point is God himself. God is our end, our good, and our way—he really is the Alpha and Omega of all things (Rev. 22:13).

As we mature from being a toddler in the faith into adolescence, we bring with us notions of the flesh still dwelling in our hearts. We still function like we are alone. We still act as if we are under the law instead of grace. We still live as if we are the source of our spiritual life. We will always be tempted to self-create a life because the lie of the garden reverberates throughout history. The original lie still tempts us that we too can be like God: We can self-live, self-create, and self-transform. It is this lie that seduces us still.

An Abiding Zeal

As we advance in the faith, especially in our spiritual adolescence, we are still tempted to hear biblical commands as a call to fix ourselves. Take, for instance, Ephesians 5:18: "Be filled with the Spirit." What is being asked of us here? In our flesh, we hear a command we can enact: "*Get filled* with the Spirit." Picking up the assumptions from our youth, we assume God has laid out a path before us and said, "Get it done!" So we run off to try to fix ourselves, turning to spiritual disciplines, ministry, and service, thinking that these are means of *getting filled*. In our adolescence, we are always looking to be filled, and so we seek to use Christian things to fill us, thinking that it is our responsibility to fill ourselves up.

At first, incredibly, it seems to work. We read the Bible and are filled with possibility and excitement. We grow in knowledge and are filled with encouragement. We engage in acts of ministry and service and are bursting with gratitude and awe. These are all good things. Praise God for these things! But one day we read our Bible and don't experience any filling. We read and feel dry. We sit down to pray and find our mind wandering to other things: life's worries, anxieties, sin, or even just the list of to-dos weighing on us. We do ministry but no longer experience the same feeling of filling. Now it seems empty.

When the Lord says, "Be filled with the Spirit," it is important to recognize that it really is a command. Interestingly, it is not an *active* command in Greek but is in the passive voice. We should hear this command as "*be* filled," and not "*get* filled." The command is not to do something that generates the filling of the Spirit. Rather, the call is to be acted upon by the Spirit. That is an entirely different reality. God is commanding us to let someone do something to us. We are commanded to let somebody fill us. To hear the command as a call to *get filled* focuses on our ability to create something rather than our activity of drawing near to God as the only one who can fill us. This is a call to abide so that we can bear much fruit because our growth is the fruit of the Spirit's filling.

If we reduce being filled with the Spirit to our activity, we seek to tether God to what we can see, like tethering God to a golden calf. We think that if we only have the right technology—doctrinal statements, spiritual practices, or liturgies—then we can harness God's power to use for our advancement. But our God is free. This is something God had to frequently remind Israel regarding the temple. No temple can contain God. God wasn't tethered to the temple, nor were its services meant to control him. God was utterly free as the consuming fire, which he reminded Israel of by consuming Nadab and Abihu right after the tabernacle was set up because they sought to use the tabernacle to harness God's power for their own ends (Lev. 10:1–3). The Lord cannot be manipulated. This is why God rebukes his people, "Do not trust in these deceptive words: 'This is the temple of the LORD, the temple of the LORD, the temple of the LORD'" (Jer. 7:4). The temple won't protect them in their folly. Their fantasy was that they could live depraved lives and then hide in the temple, thinking it would shield them from the consequences (see Matt. 21:13).

There will always be a temptation to use spiritual practices, church, and service to tether God to ourselves, thinking that as long as we do these things energetically, he will give us what we want. This misses the fact that *he* is our good, *he* is our hope, and *he* is our life. God is love, and he calls us to himself in love to be known in love. God is both our foundation for a flourishing life and the goal for a flourishing life because we truly flourish only if we embrace him. Our spiritual practices, church ministry, and service should always be ways to embrace him and offer ourselves to him. When God is not our foundation and our goal, we replace him with trying to fix our life in our own strength.

Unlike how we often understand growth in goodness and virtue, our call of obedience requires fellowship with another—with Christ. We don't simply develop spiritual virtue; we bear the fruit of abiding with Christ. This is what it means to be filled with the Spirit. We have to open our hearts to God and his work to abide in Christ, growing into him who is our head (Eph. 4:15). This means we have to recognize the ways the Word cuts us open and reveals the "thoughts and intentions" of our hearts (Heb. 4:12) and leaves us "naked and exposed" before God (v. 13). We have to stand before the Word as before a mirror and not forget what we look like (see James 1:23–24). As we see the truth, we must turn to him as our only hope and our only foundation.

What we cannot do is to turn this reality of being with God into a feeling. We cannot judge the work of God by attending to our feelings. Feeling excited or joyful does not help us discern the presence and activity of God. We have to live by faith.

Learning to Walk by Faith

To live by faith is to trust what the Lord has declared to us. This is why we cannot reduce being filled with the Spirit to a feeling. Being filled with the Spirit might feel like being abandoned. Jesus, who had the Spirit without measure, prayed, "My God, my God, why have you forsaken me?" (Matt. 27:46). Jesus sweat blood in Gethsemane as he poured out his life to the Father (Luke 22:44). Was Jesus without the Spirit? As those who pray in Jesus's name, we should not be surprised that we share these experiences with him.

With Jesus, we may find ourselves asking if God has forsaken us. With Jesus, we might have the Spirit send us into the desert to be tempted by the devil to reveal what is in our hearts (see Matt. 4:1). Like Jesus, we too will ask the Lord to take the cup of trial from us. We too struggle with where God leads us. But our feelings don't somehow locate God in the world, and they don't tell us about his presence. Rather, our feelings of struggle tell us about ourselves and the truth of how much we need him.

In 1 John 3:19–20, John explains that when we come before God, our hearts may condemn us. John locates the source of condemnation in the human heart, and yet most of us just assume God is condemning us. So we turn inward to try to change the feeling of condemnation, when the truth is that "God is greater than our heart, and he knows everything" (v. 20). The path of faith must lead us beyond what our present experience seems to be telling us—in this sense, that God is condemning us. The path of faith leads us to the God who is greater than all we experience, even

141

when our feelings tell us that he is the one condemning us. The path of faith trusts that God knows everything and that it was in our sin that he died for us. When we walk by faith, we trust that God is our true refuge, that he is where life is found, and that in him we can know joy, peace, and kindness.

Unfortunately, many assume faithfulness to the biblical commands is simply getting things done in our own power and, when we are done, saying things like "To God be the glory." We cannot imagine a different way, and so anything else feels faithless. When we read "Be filled with the Spirit," it is easy for us to subconsciously assume it is saying, "Do the right thing so that you will experience consolation." When we hear about the fruit of the Spirit, being called to love, joy, peace, patience, and such, we hear that as a command to generate these things in ourselves. Rather than understanding these as fruit of a life filled by the Spirit, we hear them as effects of our effort. We all have an incredible ability to translate the Bible's call to abide and bear the fruit of God's life as a call to create a life in our flesh. Once again, moralism lurks around every corner.

If you have put your faith in Jesus, you stand on a different foundation. Now, by having Christ, Paul says, "You were washed, you were sanctified, you were justified in the name of the Lord Jesus Christ and by the Spirit of our God" (1 Cor. 6:11). As a Christian, *you have the Spirit*. That is the truth of your life by faith. By having the Spirit, you are called to live a spiritual life—a life that seeks, rests upon, and receives the love of God poured into your heart by the Spirit (Rom. 5:5). To seek this life is to walk by faith with God in light of this truth. To be filled with the Spirit is to be caught up in God's life in the Son and to receive the love the Father has for his Son as your own (John 17:26). What this means is that you are called to the life of faith, which is life in the Spirit beyond fleshly equations.

For some, this all sounds too wonderful to be true right now. Maybe there was a time it seemed true, but you are struggling with too much to be able to say with confidence that you know the love of God. Don't try to generate faith in these moments. Don't try to fix yourself. Instead, grasp ahold of your struggle, fears, worries, and needs, and bring all of that to the Lord. Come out of hiding and tell him exactly what you are feeling and thinking and wrestling with. Be open to his forgiveness, mercy, and love.

Seeing the Heart

None of what we have said thus far will undermine how bewildering life in the desert or desolation might feel, but it can help to anchor us to Christ when we feel dry, alone, and isolated. One helpful way to explain the confusing ways of life in the Spirit is through the lens of medicine. Medicine can sometimes be painful, the cure seeming, at first, worse than the disease. So too the Spirit's ministry is often a painful work to lance the wound of our flesh to expose the truth but in the end a cure that awakens praise, gratitude, and awe from the heart.

Just as lancing a wound seems to reveal a greater problem before making it go away, the living water of the Spirit raises the vices, sin, brokenness, and pains of the heart, bringing them to the surface to show how filled we are with ourselves. This work calls us to see these things so that we can know forgiveness, redemption, and transformation *where we most need it*. If our assumption is that being filled with the Spirit will always be pleasurable, then we will miss the way the Lord is calling us to himself and exposing us to the truth.

Evangelical theologian J. I. Packer describes how this worked out in his own life. Explaining a bit of his own spiritual maturation, he writes about how oppressive the notion of being "filled with the Spirit" became for him. He began to think that being filled was something he had to make happen, and doing so could be discerned through his own experience. He writes, "All I knew was that the expected experience was not coming. The technique was not working."[1]

This led him to believe that he was not good enough. He had to cleanse himself more, work harder, and figure out a way to purify his life. He became, in his words, "fairly frantic." It was then that he came across an old Puritan classic by John Owen. In reading Owen, Packer realized that his devotion led him to a naive and undiscerning view of his own heart rather than revealing what sin really had done. He explains,

> Owen showed me my inside—my heart—as no one had ever done before. Sin, he told me, is a blind, anti-God, egocentric energy in the fallen human spiritual system, ever fomenting self-centered and self-deceiving desires, ambitions, purposes, plans, attitudes, and behaviours. Now that I was a regenerate believer, born again, a new creation in Christ, sin that formerly dominated me had been de-throned but was not yet destroyed. It was marauding within me all the time, bringing back sinful desires that I hoped I had seen the last of, and twisting my new desires for God and godliness out of shape so that they became pride-perverted too. Lifelong conflict with the besetting sins that besetting sin generates was what I must expect.[2]

What Packer explains here is what we used to call "indwelling corruption." John Owen, whom Packer was reading, explains that many people grow in such a way that they look at their lives and think, *Look! I have dealt with my lust; I no longer have that same struggle!* They think their own spiritual efforts have dealt with the problem. But, as Owen explains, the truth is often different. It is true that after decades of marriage their lust does not look the same as it did in their teenage years. However, this lust now manifests itself as pride, grandiosity, and selfish ambition.[3] While we often think of lust as simply an overactive sexual drive, it is often fueled from below by a desire to assert oneself against the grain of reality. Lust is the fruit of a heart filled with anger, grandiosity, and selfishness. Lust reveals a desire to live life on our own terms. This is how lust can mask a fountain of sin that fuels a career and how more socially acceptable sins are often fueled by springs of depravity beneath the surface.

The temptations to fill and fix oneself are significant in the Christian life. We will always be tempted to look for ways to fill ourselves and to equate God's presence, acceptance, and love with spiritual pleasure rather than trusting in the promise by faith. Whether we do this with worship, studies, service, ministry, or the quest for an experience, we are always tempted to imitate the consolation God provides by trying to use him and his gifts to secure it. Put differently, we are tempted, with the Corinthian church, to equate Christian power with worldly power and achievement, using those things to secure a life on our own terms. Instead, in the imperative "Be filled with the Spirit," we hear an invitation to draw near to the Lord who has offered himself to us, who alone can heal the soul. Come, and know the fountain of life who promises rivers of living water (see John 4:10).

EXPERIENCE

Draw near to the Lord and ask him, *When I hear, "Be filled with the Spirit," how do I hear that? Have I heard that as something I need to generate? Have I imagined that it is a certain kind of experience? Or have I just been confused and kept walking forward, hoping things would work themselves out?* Ask the Lord, *Lord, am I open to the truth that being filled with the Spirit will often reveal my flesh, giving me an experience of my flesh so that I grasp all the more onto you?*

Similarly, when you hear things like, "Be anxious for nothing" or "Do not worry about tomorrow," have those been rebukes for you to fix yourself, to try harder and get your act together, or have they been invitations to abide?

❖ *Lord, how much of my Christian experience has been about fixing myself, ridding myself of sin, and trying to manage my guilt? How am I still tempted to fix myself?*

❖ *Lord, how have I learned to interpret my experience with you? Has my interpretation led me away from you and into fantasy, or has it led me to you and into the truth?*

❖ *Lord, have I been seeking, in my own power, to "get filled" with the Spirit? What would it look like for me to be open to what the Spirit is doing instead?*

❖ *Lord, where am I now in my life with you? What are you doing in my life? What are you calling me to submit to and to lay down before you?*

❖ *Lord, where am I relying on my flesh rather than on you to live the Christian life? Fill me with your Spirit so that I can draw near to you in the truth.*

SECTION 3

Relearning the Path of Love

9

Transformed by Love

John and I understand how walking through all this can feel heavy and defeating. When we see how much of our flesh has seeped into our devotion, how much we have tried to use passion to fuel our life with God, and how we have sought moralism instead of abiding, we can feel fatigued and somewhat hopeless. But it is right here where we need to remember the depth of the good news that Christ is ours by faith. In our hopelessness we need to remember that, by faith, his righteousness is our righteousness. By faith in Jesus we have put off the flesh, we have been buried and raised with him, and the record of debt that stood against us has been nailed to the cross (Col. 2:11–14).

It is because of Christ that we can honestly admit and see how all our actions can be warped by the flesh. And so the question is, in light of the good news of Jesus, how are our lives purified? What does it look like to grow in affection rather than passion, to grow in goodness without being moralistic, and to give our lives to the Lord instead of just fixing ourselves? How do we sit in a sermon, sing, and evangelize

151

in faith, hope, and love? This gets down to the core reality of a supernatural life in Christ and not merely a natural existence, constructing a life in our own power. We do not grow by just adopting new habits to actualize our potential. We grow as we grasp ahold of Christ, making him our refuge and growing up into him who is our head (see Col. 2:19).

When we are filled with frustration, defeat, and faintheartedness, what we must remember is that Jesus knows. We have a high priest who was tempted in every way we are and yet did not sin (Heb. 4:15). We have a Lord who meets us in the darkness as one who knows the desert and the feeling of abandonment. We have a Lord who pleaded with his Father to have his cup taken from him (Matt. 26:39) and who cried out, "My God, my God, why have you forsaken me?" (27:46).

We have to remember that we are formed supernaturally in one place and in one place only: before the face of God, in Christ, by the Spirit. There is no other ground for spiritual formation than this. But we often go looking for other ground to stand on. As we've considered all the ways we seek to avoid God—in our passion, brokenness, goodness, devotion, and action to fix ourselves—we've seen that we are tempted to self-focus rather than seek God and his kingdom first. We're often afraid that if we don't actualize ourselves and make something of ourselves, then no one will uphold us and our life will come apart. We fail to really know—all the way down—that in losing our lives for Christ we find them. In laying down our lives, we can know that our lives are "hidden with Christ in God" (Col. 3:3).

Spiritual Formation in Reality

The mistake we might make as we are confronted with how fleshly our Christian lives still are is to trade purification and maturation with the fantasy that we can just actualize ourselves. But spiritual formation looks different from this. Spiritual formation requires that we start where we actually are—in our guilt, shame, fear, and anxiety but also in our pride, jealousy, and greed—and draw near to the God who is perfect love. We draw near because of what he has done and because we are no longer defined by sin and brokenness but by Christ and his righteousness.

Stop for a moment before you read on and ponder what was just said. We should not pass this by quickly. Spiritual formation requires us to pause and see the truth, naming how our guilt, shame, fear, and anxiety have led us, and also the various ways our pride, jealousy, and greed still infiltrate our decisions. We need to see and name these things to draw near to the God who is perfect love. We repent and draw near to God in Christ Jesus who died for us, trusting by faith that it is by his wounds that we are healed (1 Pet. 2:24). Hear this call:

1. Come to God *just as you are, in the messy truth of your life.* Come in the truth of your sin and brokenness, and call out to the Lord in the unvarnished reality of your life, just as we see in the Psalms.

2. Do not merely draw near to the idea of God, but draw near to God himself in the truth of his love, mercy, grace, and forgiveness. Meet him as he is, in light of who you are.

3. Do this because he has offered you forgiveness and love and not because you loved him first.

4. In doing so, draw near to him in Christ, recalling that your deepest identity is no longer a broken sinner but one who is *loved, forgiven, and clothed in Christ's*

righteousness. Come as a child of your heavenly Father.

This is the pattern of our life in Christ and in the Spirit. Right now, pause and open your heart to God as described in those four steps. Remember that you cannot transform yourself, but you can open your life to the One who can. Do not read on until you try what the Scriptures encourage us to do. Take a chance, stop, and open your heart to this—even if just for a few moments. Taste and see what it is to trust him and his work and words. If you do not want to do this, tell the Lord. Even in that place you are finally opening to him in the truth.

When we avoid drawing near to the Lord this way, we are tempted not to come out of hiding, and we are in danger of living our lives relying on passion for motivation or responding moralistically to attain faithfulness. This is the temptation to live the Christian life alone rather than in communion with him. However, seeing the truth that life in the flesh does not work can feel debilitating. We might feel frozen. When we're used to fixing ourselves and we learn that we can't, sometimes we just give up and assume there is nothing left for us to do. *If I can't grow myself,* we think, *I must not have to do anything.* But this is not the path of faith either.

Bernard of Clairvaux, one of Protestantism's favorite ancient spiritual writers, saw what happened to Christians when they lost sight of faith, hope, and love. Bernard lamented that too many Christians in his day had become like canals who immediately poured out whatever they received. Today, we might say that they go right from reading something to posting it online, only to move on to the next thing immediately afterward. A canal gives away what it does not yet fully own. A canal is always giving but never growing, increasingly consumed and shallow rather than deep and full.

Instead of canals, Bernard claims, we need people who are reservoirs. A reservoir is someone filled to overflowing. A reservoir is a person who is filled with the Spirit and is being filled with wisdom, knowledge, and love, who then pours those forth in all they do. The image of a reservoir recognizes that Christian growth is something we first receive from God but then must allow to fill us. This image recognizes that spiritual practices open us up to love himself, and form us in love and for love.

Purified in Love

To become a reservoir, one must embrace a life with Jesus that is receiving and reciprocating—receiving God's life and responding by offering him ours. And yet, one of the repeated refrains in the spiritual formation movement is that spiritual practices cannot transform us, leaving some to wonder why they should bother with them at all. *If they don't transform me, why am I doing them?* Most people, of course, don't just ignore spiritual practices. Most Christians happily go to church, read their Bible, pray, and engage in other spiritual practices. But the temptation is to forget that the goal of our practices is to lead us into the purifying presence of God and to instead imagine that as long as we do the right practices in the right ways, we will be transformed. The problem is that we can easily affirm that spiritual practices cannot form us while simultaneously assuming they do. In other words, the danger in focusing on spiritual disciplines is that we can come to believe Christianity is basically like the formation of our bodies at the gym. We think, *Maybe I've just been working out in the wrong way!*

It is, of course, important to consider our spiritual practices and the overall rhythms of our lives. But instead of focusing on all the things you are not doing, we want you to pause and consider what you already are doing because you are a Christian. There are standard practices, what we used to call the normal "means of grace," that are meant to give shape to the Christian life. These means of grace are things like going to church, devotionally reading Scripture, praying, meditating, and serving. Instead of just thinking about these things, bring them to the Lord. *Lord, what fuels my church-going? What drives my service? What do I embrace as a calling on my life, and what do I avoid?*

Instead of assuming you are not doing enough, it is important to start with the things you are doing and consider with the Lord, *Lord, how are you purifying these things that I am doing in your love?* Ask, *Lord, what would it look like to do all these things in gratitude based on what you have done for me and the grace you have given me?* If I'm not grateful, can I come to God in that truth and seek him who is faithful? Attend to how you might use your Christian practices not to draw near to God but to be good (moralism), to get excited (passion), or just to get life on your own terms (fixing yourself). Instead, intend something different with him: *Lord, I want you. I don't want to just fix myself. I don't want to use you and the things you have given to fix my life. I want what you want for me. I want to abide in you wherever you lead.* As you do so, do not be surprised when parts of you say, "Yes!" and other parts of you call you a liar and refuse to believe that God is this gracious. Now bring that to him too.

In all this, our drawing near to the Lord should be conformed to the prayer, "I believe; help my unbelief" (Mark 9:24). By resting in the fact that he is our righteousness, we have space to see the truth of our unbelief and all the ways we avoid God in our passion, goodness, devotion, and such. We need to know God's grace and mercy in these places just as we need to hear the Lord's calling and direction out of our sin and brokenness to be formed in his love. But we should never hear the call away from our sin and brokenness apart from Christ. This means we have to constantly reframe our experiences in light of who Christ is and what he has done and in light of who we are in him by grace through faith.

The clear biblical call is to bear the fruit of our abiding in Christ and not merely to generate growth. Our call is to be transformed in Christ's embrace of us as we, by faith, embrace him back. What this means is that the goal of our action is not simply to stop doing bad things and replace them with good things. There is a deeper truth. The call of spiritual formation is to become the kind of person who, when pierced, bleeds forgiveness, grace, and mercy like our Lord. Our Lord is the One who, while being beaten and killed, prayed, "Father, forgive them, for they know not what they do" (Luke 23:34). The goal is to so embrace Christ and make him our refuge that our life is conformed to his. But the only way to walk this path is through the truth of our lives, hearts, and bodies. We must present ourselves to him in light of what our life has been, what it is, and what we long for it to be in Christ.

We miss the significance of drawing near and abiding when we reduce spiritual formation to practicing certain spiritual disciplines. When this happens, we can develop new habits, new rhythms, or new actions and still not have a transformed life. Enacting new habits is not enough. We are not called to "fake it till we make it" or to try hard to *act* like good Christians. Formation is not achieved through raw effort. Our formation is the fruit of God's life in our lives. God calls us to a new foundation of life—the Spirit's presence in the soul and among his people—wanting to transform the deepest parts of our hearts by reorienting all of us in him and to him so that we can bear the fruit of the kingdom.

This is where we discover a hard tension in the Christian life. Even though spiritual formation is never simply habit formation, we still have to develop habits that will reveal his power in our weakness (see 2 Cor. 12:9). Spiritual formation is not the fruit of self-effort, but you'll still need to give effort. Spiritual formation is not primarily oriented to your formation, but you'll still need to give yourself to your formation. This is what often confuses people about the Christian life. The reason for these tensions is that the Christian life is formation by the grace of God.

A New Foundation: Moving from Rest

The new foundation we have received from God is holiness and love, as we are indwelled by the Spirit of holiness who pours forth love into our hearts (Rom. 5:5). When we engage in a spiritual practice, the ground from which we move is not our abilities, strength, or savvy but the Spirit. We should not fuel our spiritual efforts with passion or find the ground of our spiritual stance in ourselves. There is no foothold in ourselves; there is only shifting sand in autonomy. The only ground we have is Christ by his grace. We come in the truth of our lives and move from grace, which is an entirely new foundation from which to act. This foundation is rest, which is established by God's work of salvation. So we move not from anxious toiling but from the rest that God has secured. Christ is the foundation and ground of our spiritual growth.

Moving from rest and not from our own works has always been ingrained in God's people. This was at the heart of

Sabbath. The Lord declared to his people, "Above all you shall keep my Sabbaths, for this is a sign between me and you throughout your generations, that you may know that I, the LORD, sanctify you" (Exod. 31:13). The Lord is the One who sanctifies his people. In him we receive holiness and do not generate it through our action. We are always first receivers of God's life and grace and mercy. He establishes peace. It is from resting in him and trusting in his work that we respond. Our insufficiency and his sufficiency are the ground upon which we came to him in the first place, and they are the ground upon which we always stand in the Christian life.

We know this foundation from God within us, but we know it by faith, and we cannot locate it through our senses (we walk by faith and not by sight). In early consolation we imagine we can equate his presence with *having an experience* of God's presence. But we cannot. God shows us that his presence sometimes awakens condemnation in our souls (see 1 John 3:19–20) and that sometimes he gives thorns in the flesh as gifts (see 2 Cor. 12:1–10). These are effects of God being with us, even though we often interpret them as his being absent.

Because of the nature of our life with Christ, faith is not something we simply start the Christian life with. We must *walk by faith*, and it is only by faith that we know who we are.

We are the redeemed.

We are beloved.

We are his children.

We are those who can rest in the peace he has established. But this rest does not, or should not, lead to passivity any more than marriage should lead away from growing in love. Rather, it is the context for love and the context for growth.

159

This is where we start: the new foundation given by God that allows us to move from rest. This means we are never generating goodness, establishing holiness, or fixing our lives. We are always receiving. He has given himself to us, and so we give ourselves to him. To grow in grace, therefore, requires that we do not use spiritual practices to establish a new foundation or to recover consolation that we then use as a foundation for our action. Starting with rest is laying down all of our desires to establish our own rest or to get out of the desert or avoid desolation. Walking by faith is presenting ourselves to him and trusting him wherever he leads.

So as you are sitting in a sermon, reading the Word, praying, or ministering to others, ask what it might look like to do these as a way of standing upon the foundation he has laid. What would it mean to do these things as a way of responding to God's kindness? What would it mean to engage in these things as a way of first receiving from him and then responding to that reception? Maybe more importantly, and easier to miss, what would it mean to do these things as a way to be watchful of your heart (see Col. 4:2) and to see how much of what you are doing is actually fleshly? We want to be reservoirs filled to overflowing and not canals that remain shallow because we are never being filled. We want to receive first and not simply act, because our hope and our growth come from God.

A New Purpose: Living in Peace

In modern terms, we often use peace as the opposite of war. But there is a deeper sense of peace we find in Scripture. The idea of shalom in Scripture is not simply that war has ceased but that God's presence and action bring order, harmony, and flourishing. When we seek to draw near to God in our actions—meditating, listening to a sermon, singing, serving, fasting—we are moving from rest into his peace. We recognize that we are discordant notes in the symphony of God's kingdom and that he is tuning our hearts to sing his praise.

Unlike the training we undergo for sports, where there is a set of skills we seek to cultivate, to thrive in the kingdom of God requires something deeper. You can be an incredible athlete and a terrible person. You can, in Jesus's words, gain the world and lose your soul (Matt. 16:26). Training for life in the kingdom, instead, is a whole-life harmonizing around "the beauty of holiness" (Ps. 29:2 NKJV). This is training for life in the presence of God, where we receive him, rest in him, and embrace what he calls good, holy, and true. The training of the Christian life involves receiving God and his kingdom and, through his grace, walking into his reign and rule as the proper way to see the world. This is a training in wisdom. It is a life of one planted by streams of water, thriving wherever God plants you (Ps. 1:3).

We do not achieve this through spiritual practices themselves; our action does not just form the kingdom in us. Rather, through spiritual practices, we are taking a step into the unseen reign of God and walking into his presence as a way to affirm the truth of who he is and what he has done. This is why our spiritual life is an entire life and not merely a set of disciplines: We are called to become a certain kind of person, *a person who flourishes in the presence of God.*

All of life can be lived in the rest and peace of God. All of life can now be lived in response to what God has done for us. If this life feels burdensome, then draw near to God in Christ by the Spirit. If you feel bored, come to him as one who is bored in his presence, trusting that you are received in him and by him, not because of your goodness but because of his steadfast love and mercy. Spiritual practices should always be funded by the rest he provides, but they also need to conform to the contours of his life. We are saved for him, to know life with him, so that we can walk in him.

To walk and live in his peace means that we are not trying to establish our own order or our own kingdom. We are submitting to him and his way. This also means that we are not using spiritual practices to somehow create a life or persona we imagine is worthwhile, as if the goal of spiritual practices is to feel centered, whole, or non-anxious. This might become true, but it is not the goal. These feelings often seduce us into achieving something we can create in ourselves rather than using these practices to lay down our lives to Christ.

Our calling is to embrace Christ and his life and to walk in his way. This is the path for flourishing in his kingdom, and it still requires that we "make every effort" to do so (2 Pet. 1:5–7). Our formation is not passive. As Dallas Willard writes, "Grace is opposed to earning, not to effort."[1] This is true. However, our formation is not by willpower or effort alone but through our union and communion with God, in Christ, by the power of his Spirit (see Eph. 3:16–19).[2] This is the formation of love because love binds our hearts together with Christ's and forms us in his presence and by his presence. Our lives need to be conformed to Christ. This is not something done against us but is what happens as we embrace him by the Spirit.

A New Goal: Abiding in Love

As a training in love, our focus begins with God, the God who is love (1 John 4:8). By his grace, he has offered himself to you in love and for love. This means that the proper goal of our spiritual practices—the true end to which our life and actions should point—is God himself. He is our goal, and in abiding in him we bear much fruit, for apart from him we can do nothing (John 15:5).

When we understand that the calling of the Christian is to abide to bear fruit, we can see that the call in every season is the same—to draw near. This is why we are called to present our bodies as living sacrifices (Rom. 12:1). We draw near to the Lord and offer ourselves to the Lord. Only in doing so do we grow "with a growth that is *from God*" (Col. 2:19, emphasis added). But drawing near means we do so in light of the brokenness, sin, and depravity of our souls. It means seeing our jealousy as we stand before the Holy One in the truth. It means seeing our greed, lust, and grandiosity before the face of the One who gave himself for us. To walk by faith is to see the truth and take it to the one place where healing is actually found—in Christ.

This is the surprising logic of the kingdom: If you try to save your life, you will lose it. Likewise, the same is true with spiritual practices: If you use them to grow, you will lose sight of Jesus. If you try to form yourself, you will do exactly that, self-formation. But if you abide in him, grasping his life and making him your refuge, you will discover life in him. The formation we are called to is the Spirit's work to form us into the likeness of Jesus. This happens face-to-face with him as we draw near in the truth of our lives.

We need to attend—in consolation, in the desert, and in desolation—to what we are being shown by the Lord about our spiritual practices. Are we just trying to make life work? Have our spiritual practices become the equivalent of self-help or life hacks? Are these practices actually revealing the deep truths of our hearts and leading us to abide in him, or are they leading us to abide in ourselves? We don't need to be afraid of seeing the truth because Christ is the ground of our formation, the archetype of our growth, and the goal of our activity.

Beyond Willpower by Faith: Supernatural Growth

In all of our spiritual practices, and in all of life, we are to move from his rest and peace to abide in his love. This is spiritual formation that stands on our justification by grace through faith. This is the historic vision of Protestantism: a spiritual formation that is by grace alone, through faith alone, in Christ alone, for the glory of God alone.[3] This is the vision that embraces the truth that only when we lose our lives do we find them, but to find them in Christ is to know the truth of human flourishing and the peace of God that is beyond understanding. This is the formation of a Christian in love and by love, beyond anxious toiling, because it is a formation secured in Christ who is our sanctification (see 1 Cor. 1:30).

Our willpower is not enough for our formation. We need another—Jesus—by his Spirit, in order to bear the fruit of his life. In the words of Dallas Willard, "Christian spiritual formation is focused entirely on Jesus. Its goal is an obedience or conformity to Christ that arises out of an inner transformation accomplished through purposive interaction with the grace of God in Christ."[4] Our training is in faith, hope, and love, as it is the training of those who are living their lives in harmony with and in reliance on Jesus. This means that patience, peace, joy, kindness, and all other virtues are given shape in us only as we make him our rest, peace, and refuge. Becoming patient in the Spirit is not the same as becoming patient in the flesh. Bearing the fruit of patience is being with our Lord as we lay down our life to him, willing life with him instead of life in our flesh. It is only through this union with him that we are spiritually formed.

At the heart of this vision of spiritual formation is that it is only available by faith. The sad truth is that I (Kyle) learned the opposite growing up in the church. What I internalized, although no one taught me specifically, was that I needed faith to become a Christian, but the goal was never to live by faith. Instead of living by faith, I was offered all sorts of ways to live by sight. I was given things to do that I could focus on, and I was told that doing them was focusing on God.

To become reservoirs pouring over rather than canals, we must be filled with love from the God who did everything needed to embrace us as his own. He doesn't send us away to grow now that he has forgiven us. He does not send the Spirit to empower a self-formed life. He sends his Spirit to unite us to himself so we can grow with a growth from God. He calls us to himself in the truth of our neediness so that we can be filled by his love.

Do You Love Me?

It turns out that the path of love is a hard one to navigate. Maturation in love invites us into places in our hearts and lives that we would rather ignore. We need to draw near to the Lord, but our fleshly formation blinds us to this, leading us away from acknowledging the truth. The Lord, just as he did with Peter after his resurrection, calls us into his love by leading us through places of our sin, shame, and brokenness, guiding us into vistas of healing where we truly need it. The Lord asks Peter three times, "Simon, son of John, do you love me?" (John 21:15–17), recalling Peter's three denials of his Lord. The Lord wanted Peter to feel his failure in the presence of the Lord's love for him.

But there is more going on in Jesus's interaction with Peter. In Jesus's kindness, he wanted Peter to know that Peter did in fact love Jesus, even in his weakness and frailty.[5] He also wanted Peter to hear his calling in his brokenness and sin so that he would not be tempted to hope in his own goodness but in the steadfast love and mercy of the Lord. Confronted with our own failure, we would often rather just mumble a confession and move on, whereas the Lord leads us into the truth so we can know the depth of his forgiveness.

It seems that Peter learned this lesson well. Much later, Peter reminds us of the danger of forgetting that we have been cleansed from our former sins (2 Pet. 1:9). Peter knew the truth that it was only in remembering this and seeing our sins for what they are that we can embrace ever more deeply the love of the Lord. The Lord knows, and the Lord calls us to himself in and through our brokenness, sin, and pain to abide in him to bear much fruit. The only way to mature in love is through abiding honestly with him because the way of love calls us into the truth. This is obvious on paper, but it is entirely counterintuitive to our experiences and assumptions. Freedom in Christ is not often what we think until we discover it is deeper than we dared imagine.

To grow in love requires that we come to the Lord as he truly is in light of who we truly are. As Christians, we are in Christ Jesus—redeemed, reconciled, and saved—and yet we come in the truth of what has happened in our lives, what sin remains, and what ways we are being deceived by the corruption within us. This means that to walk by the Spirit will require us to grapple with our sinful deception, our worldly desires, and the ways our flesh longs to assert itself. We need to know God's love right where we need it—in our brokenness, sin, and shame—as we present our bodies as living sacrifices to the One who has called us to himself. This path of love is a humbling one, but it is the only path where true life is found.

Instead of rushing to add on a bunch of practices in hopes of fixing your life, start with what you already give yourself to, but now do it from within God's rest, peace, and love to present yourself to him in love. Be watchful of the ways you want to manage God or manipulate him, and watch all the ways your heart wants to turn God into a path of fixing your life. Lay down all the things that lead you away from him and draw near to your Lord, and trust that as you do so, he will form you increasingly into his likeness.

EXPERIENCE

Open your heart to the Lord and pray to him:

❖ *Lord, how am I tempted to make the Christian life about my growth rather than about you and being with you?*

❖ *Lord, how am I tempted, like the Galatians were, to begin with the Spirit but continue with the flesh? How am I tempted to use my spiritual disciplines, faithfulness, or resources to construct a life instead of abandoning my life to you?*

❖ *Lord, here are some of the broken and sinful pieces of my heart—my worry, anger, and hatred. Father, forgive me. Teach me, God, and help me to know your love in these places. Help me not to be afraid to bring you the truth of my life, and keep me from trying to fix these in my own power.*

Take a moment to come as you are to the Lord, sharing both sins and struggles, and hear him ask you, as he did Peter, "Do you love me?" Come to him in the parts of you that shout "Yes!" as well as in the parts that struggle to know.

❖ *Lord, I present myself to you. Right now, I present my body to you as a living sacrifice. My Father, here I am. God, I am yours. Lord, I need you. Have mercy on me, and help me abide in you in the truth.*

10

Walking the Path Ahead

The good news of salvation is that God has given himself to you in Christ Jesus. He has done everything needed so that you can have life in him and with him by the Spirit. Christ is your salvation.[1] The life Scripture calls us to is a life of holiness and love—lived by grace through faith in the truth of who we are. In light of this, the unique training we are called to undertake is life in the presence of God and for the presence of God. Put differently, our training is always a training in him and with him. This is a training of love. Because of this, as we see throughout all Scripture, Christian growth is often confusing. In particular, it is our experience of life with God interpreted through our intentions and expectations that we feel such confusion.

The reason our intentions often blind us is that they become lenses we look through to interpret our behavior. When we look through our good intentions, even our failures are given a rose-colored shading. When our intent *feels* strong, we blind ourselves to how broken and even sinful our actions really are. A really strong intention to be faithful often makes our sinfulness and brokenness appear less rebellious. Like the Pharisees who couldn't love much because they didn't know how much they needed forgiveness, our intentions can easily numb us to our desperate need for grace.

Similar to our intentions, our expectations color our experiences, often leading us away from interpreting them by faith. When we expect that we will experience consolation if we are zealous enough or that we will continue to conquer sin after sin after sin as long as we remain disciplined, our expectations lead us to believe that the desert and desolation are things we can fix in our own power. Our expectations, just like the disciples' expectations concerning Jesus, often lead us away from him rather than to rest in him.

Obedient from the Heart

As we grow, the Lord leads us to trust that we are safest in his hands and plans and not our own. He knows our fears, worries, joys, loves, and struggles, and he is not afraid of them as we are. He knows the ways we struggle to draw near to him, as well as the places in our hearts that feel too broken, tainted, and rebellious to bring to him. Yet he calls us near. He calls us by name in the truth of our life. He calls us to abide in him, to come and draw deeply from a well that never runs dry, especially when our hearts feel dry as dust.

Our experiences suggest other things are true. In our flesh, we become convinced that the paths of healing are the very paths we must protect ourselves against. Or, in our spiritual immaturity, we become convinced that we have to grow ourselves in our own power or just sit around until God "zaps us" with growth.[2] Likewise, some come to believe that if they just adopt the "right" spiritual practices, then God will be happy with them and give them the life they want. This seems to work in consolation, but as life goes on, the Lord shows them the truth of their heart and all seems broken and confusing.

Thankfully, our life does not follow a simple (1) consolation, (2) desert, and (3) desolation trajectory. But it is important to understand what these seasons are for. Our call is not to generate an experience or get out of desolation but to inquire of the Lord about what it means to be faithful and obedient from the heart. If you are in consolation, praise God! Draw near to him and discern with him what faithfulness looks like in this season. In later seasons of consolation, we are being taught, with Paul, what it is like to be in seasons of abundance and lack (see Phil. 4:10–13). In both of these seasons we are learning that "I can do all things through him who strengthens me" (v. 13).

Instead of consolation, maybe you find yourself in the desert. Don't try to get out of the desert. Don't try to fix your life. Instead, offer yourself to the Lord and seek to walk by faith. Allow him to open your heart to the truth and show you all that is within you. This is what the Lord does in the desert. Draw near to him and trust that he is always with you. You can still tell him that you long for consolation or that you desperately want out of the desert. Bring your longings to the Lord in the shape of Jesus's prayer, "Not my will, but yours, be done" (Luke 22:42).

If you find yourself in desolation, remember that desolation is an opportunity to stand before God, not only in the reality of bad and sinful decisions we sometimes make but in the truth of what our character has become. When I (John) first experienced desolation, I resisted and tried to create consolation because I didn't think God could be with me in the badness of my life. No one else wanted to be with me in all my junk, so I figured God didn't either. But this thinking has to be transformed. God doesn't just ignore our badness, brokenness, and rebellion. He wants to transform us into the kinds of people who, when pierced, bleed the fruit of the Spirit.

One of the first things I learned in desolation was that no amount of right willing can minimize it because desolation is not an issue of the will. I already wanted to do the things of God. I didn't want to be sinful. I didn't want to be rebellious. When I woke up in the morning, my will said, "Let's be faithful to God today!" Yet there were sin and brokenness internal to my character. So when the Spirit pierced my heart to show me the truth, I responded by covering it up. I didn't think God wanted to see the very thing he was opening in me. I learned that my calling in this was to draw near to him in the truth. This is something for you to sit with. *Can I be with the Lord in the truth? Can I be with him in the places I might not even be honest with myself about?*

As you walk in the desert or in desolation, one thing the Lord is revealing to you is what has fueled your spiritual practices. Some realize they have been fueling their Bible reading through grandiosity. Others long for the pleasure of their passion, and so they love the exhilaration of worship more than the God they are worshiping. For things like prayer, especially, we come to discover that the consolation of pleasure rather than a desire to be with our God in reality has fueled our prayer. When consolation is taken away, our wills begin to struggle. Kyle and I have met many seminary students who simply stopped praying because consolation waned. Since consolation had been propping up their prayer life, now the practice of prayer began to mirror their lack of formation. This is an opportunity to present yourself to the

Lord: *Lord, prayer feels dead to me right now. Lord, I need you. Be with me here, Father.*

This is why our growth requires that we attend to *how* we practice what we do and honestly recognize what we long for in and through our devotion. Are we longing for God, or are we simply looking to feel better? When you go to pray or practice a discipline, and you feel the bottom drop out and the gas tank goes down to *E*, remember that the goal is not to supercharge your will to get it done. The goal is to go to God and say, *God, I need YOU.*

Some experience their will falling flat, and they just stop praying. Instead of turning to God, they turn away. But now we can see that desolation is an opportunity to draw near to God in the truth. This is an invitation to abide. As when we watched the water drain out of the lake, we can see this either as ruining our day of sailing or as a new opportunity to be with the Lord. In desolation, the gift of the Lord is to learn John 15: *Jesus, you are the vine; I am not. My willpower is not the vine that gives me life. You are the vine, and I am just a branch. Help me abide in you. Apart from you I can do nothing* (our paraphrase).

The gift of desolation is this lesson: We can do nothing apart from God. This is where we learn, from our gut, that God's power is made perfect in our weakness (2 Cor. 12:9). This is not an abstract notion but something we learn with God as he leads us into this season. At the bottom of our hearts we are learning to say, *God, I cannot do this.* But if we hear this in the flesh, we are in a terrible danger. Here, we are an inch away from either returning to the nagging of our moralistic efforts or moving to a despair where our will deflates entirely. This is why we must seek God: *God, I cannot do this apart from you. God, I don't even want to try. I want you.* Like the trembling child who says, "Mom, I can't sleep," we too need to seek the Lord in our fears, worries, and anxieties, trusting that he is our refuge. Even if our prayer is, *Lord, I don't even want to pray; Lord be with me*, then we will really be talking and walking with him.

Five Paths

We have no doubt that this book has raised many different sorts of questions, and so we want you to choose your own path forward. Below we offer five paths you can take that specifically address questions that may have emerged in your reading of this book. Here we lay out topics and questions these paths address.

Some of you might be thinking, *Why have I never heard this before?* This is an important question. You might be asking it with a bit of incredulity: *If this is true, why hasn't anyone told me about this?* Some might be asking it out of anger: *Why am I just hearing this now?* It is important not to skip over a question like this. Nothing we said in this book is new. All these things have been taught by Christians broadly and in our own Protestant tradition more narrowly. Unfortunately, over the past several generations, we have lost touch with our Christian family history. So we wanted to provide you with some examples of folks who have struggled with these same issues. Therefore, path 1 narrates how several Protestant pastor-theologians have understood developmental growth, consolation, and desolation.

While the main focus of this book has been on how individual Christians experience seasons of consolation, the desert, and desolation and the kinds of training we are called to throughout them, the second path considers how the church experiences these seasons. This is significant to consider because how we respond to these experiences corporately will have a major impact on how individuals interpret them. Importantly, this is a question not only for those who lead churches but for all of us who participate in the body of Christ. We need to consider how we navigate the various seasons the Lord leads us through both individually and corporately.

The third path you can take is of spiritual theology. This has been a book about spiritual theology by two professors of spiritual theology. Our students at the Institute for Spiritual Formation come to us because they want to wrestle through what life with God is actually like. They learn the Bible and theology like all seminary students, but our unique focus is on the formation of the student. Our goal is to walk with students in and through transformation with the Lord as they draw near to him in a community committed to a deeper life with God. You may wonder if there are more steps to take down this path, and so we will explain a bit more about what those might look like. Likewise, if you feel a call to walk with others down this path or wonder how you can help shepherd others as they walk through consolation, the desert, and desolation, we will explain more about that as well.

The fourth path talks specifically to folks who are in full-time or part-time ministry. If you find yourself working in leadership, in the church, on the mission field, or in a Christian parachurch organization, we want to reflect a bit on your unique struggle. It is profoundly difficult to walk with the Lord, particularly in the desert and desolation, when you are being paid to "do ministry." Too often folks internalize the idea that they have to look like they never struggle or appear like they always have their act together, and they end up slowly dying inside. Or folks are tempted to endlessly explore these struggles and never seem to find resolution, leaving them and the people they teach more confused than before. We want to invite you into something deeper.

Fifth, because of how difficult and confusing the desert and desolation can be, we provide some general pastoral wisdom for folks walking through these seasons. Our own Protestant tradition has always worried that people won't have someone to guide them in these seasons or that they will simply turn inward and get lost in themselves and not understand that their experience is a normal part of maturation. Our hope in this section is to offer you a framework for navigating these seasons by faith. This path can be a place to return to in order to recall the main themes and directions of what we have shared in this book. We hope it will be a guide to remember our call to turn to the Lord in all things.

Ultimately, our invitation to you in this book has been a simple one: Draw near to your Lord. Seek him with your whole heart. Do not be afraid of what you experience in yourself and in your life with him, but draw near to him in faith, hope, and love. Trust that your life is at its safest and most secure in him and with him. Finally admit fully that trusting in yourself does not bring rest and peace. You have nothing to lose in drawing near to God, and you have everything to gain. This is as true in your maturing as it was in your conversion. Seek the Lord in faith, wherever he leads.

Some of you may not need to choose a path because you have plenty to sit with right now. What you might need is more direct guidance for drawing near to the Lord. Our previous book, *Where Prayer Becomes Real: How Honesty with God Transforms Your Soul*, is a good next step. The focus of that book is on drawing near to God and abiding, and it offers practical guidance for how to do so. Alongside this, you can also check out our introductory course on spiritual formation, where I (John) walk through the material of this book (and more). Check it out at https://www.learn.biola.edu/bundles/the-journey-phase-1.

Path 1:
Why Have I Never Heard This Before?

When John and I teach on consolation and desolation, students typically respond with "Why have I never heard this before?" Because many of our students come out of an evangelicalism that has forgotten its own tradition, the temptation is to think we are introducing something foreign and alien to evangelical spirituality. But this is far from the truth. In fact, it is everywhere in the Protestant spiritual tradition. We are not going to attempt to give you a full accounting of the Protestant tradition on consolation and desolation but instead want to point out key resources to our own tradition on the topic.

For instance, William Gurnall (1616–1679), the great Puritan spiritual writer, claims that "The Christian must *trust in a withdrawing God*," adding, "Let him that walks in darkness, and sees no light, trust in the name of the Lord, and stay upon his God."[3] The notion that God withdraws has been addressed through varying terminology. The term that has lasted the longest is the "dark night of the soul." This name, associated with the work of John of the Cross, was sometimes used by Protestants. Whereas straightforward biblical language to describe God's absence, such as "the desert," was normally employed, Protestants often used the

177

language of "spiritual desertion." *Desertion* was the God-given experience of God's absence, which was understood as an experience of isolation, loneliness, and even forsakenness.

In his wonderful book about meditating on Jesus, Protestant pastor-theologian Isaac Ambrose (1604–1664) claims that in desertion, a Christian searches but finds nothing of Jesus. In other words, the Christian feels forsaken. Although Christ will never actually forsake a Christian, "the acts of his love may be withdrawn, but his love is still the same, it is 'an everlasting love,' Jeremiah 31:3."[4] Notice here that the calling of desertion is to know, by faith, that God's love is steadfast. This is an invitation to draw near to the Lord to offer oneself to him in truth, and yet that does not take away the difficulty of the experience. Sometimes the Lord offers consolation and sometimes the desert or desolation, but the goal ends up being the same—to call the believer to draw near to him and seek him.

Almost universally, the Protestant tradition has one major worry about desertion: that Christians will question if they have true faith at all and wonder if they have ever been saved. In other words, these writers were most often worried about Christians despairing in their desolation. Francis Rous (1579–1659), a member of the Westminster Assembly, worried about how Satan would use desertion to lead people to themselves rather than to the Lord and was concerned that they wouldn't find someone knowledgeable about the spiritual life to guide them. His advice: "When the soul is in the dark, and her own light shines not, she may do well to get a guide, and to take heed to borrowed light, until the day dawn, and the day-star arise in her own heart."[5] Find a Christian who can help buoy your soul with proper guidance and instruction to trust in the Lord's faithfulness and not your own current experience.

Even more developed is the account from another pastor-theologian, this time in the Dutch Reformed tradition, Wilhelmus à Brakel (1635–1711). Part of the education in spirituality, for à Brakel, was learning that "growth which does not center in Christ is no spiritual growth" at all.[6] Attending to the early years of the spiritual life, he writes, "The initial zeal of the believer is mixed with many natural passions."[7] Likewise, in reflecting on the experience of living in this early consolation and the immaturity that comes with it, he explains that many end up making poor decisions in these seasons. "We then know neither when nor how to act," he claims, and explains how this season leads to an unstable Christian existence.[8] It is "tossed by the waves," to use a biblical image (see Eph. 4:14). It is only "after frequent stumblings, falling and rising again, [that] we then begin to walk more steadfastly, rely more upon the Lord Jesus by faith—even when the Lord hides Himself, and the feelings, which the Christian is so intent upon having, depart."[9]

Here we see à Brakel wrestling with the same material we did in the first part of this book. Early in the Christian life, a believer is often filled with both zeal and natural passion (which is too often equated with supernatural affection). Even minor events can send us spinning. Notice that à Brakel is implicitly contrasting this with maturity, which is more stable and less chaotic. As we mature and the Lord leads us into places where he hides himself, we are now able to walk with him in the dark.

As he continues, à Brakel calls Christians to bring themselves into the presence of God to name the truth of their heart. In doing so, however, he warns them about their ability to judge themselves, saying, "Many are not capable of perceiving their own growth."[10] Part of the problem, he notes, is that Christians have "spiritual winters," where it seems like everything has died.[11] À Brakel is not satisfied with a general account of a "spiritual winter" but details our experiences in the Christian life in a profoundly nuanced way. He writes about spiritual backsliding, spiritual desertion, spiritual darkness, and spiritual deadness, carefully distinguishing each condition and noting how each shows up in the life of a believer.

In the case of spiritual backsliding, he turns first to encouragement. One of the first temptations is to think we are the only one to experience these things, which leads us to imagine we have never been saved.[12] If we allow ourselves to think this way, he worries it will exacerbate the struggle that has already occurred in our lives. Explaining backsliding, which occurs when the Christian begins to give up on drawing near to God or rejecting their sin, à Brakel explains that God

> wishes to acquaint them, in a vivid and experiential manner, with His longsuffering, the freeness of His grace, His care for them, and His faithfulness. To that end He occasionally withdraws Himself, even though there are no specific reasons given from their side. At least this is not the reason for His withdrawal. Observe this, for example, in 2 Chronicles 32:31: "God left him (Hezekiah), to try him, that he might know all that was in his heart."[13]

À Brakel worries that the backsliding Christian who turned to Christ for help early in life now imagines they should be beyond this kind of dependence. Through the early development in consolation, the believer had internalized the notion that they needed Christ initially for salvation but came to believe that Christ now wants them to figure it out on their own. So instead of abiding—instead of acting *from*

God and *for* God—they seek to self-generate the Christian life to their demise. When this happens, because they feel the weight of the Christian life, they give themselves to it vigorously. What we might assume is odd, however, is that it seems to work! This is what we have called "pumping up the will." They immediately see what seems like good fruit and think, *This is great, I'm growing.* "In reality," à Brakel explains, "they remain immature and even regress from the measure of spirituality they previously had."[14]

When à Brakel turns to desertion, he gives an important qualification: "Among all the ways in which the Lord leads His people, *spiritual desertion* is among the most unique. Believers generally do not behave themselves well when thus led," he claims.[15] Desertion can happen at any time throughout a believer's life, sometimes at the beginning and sometimes at the end, but one great temptation in this season is to think you can fix it. In this sense, à Brakel warns, the believer has not yet learned the truth of their own spiritual impotence: "They secretly imagine that all will come to rights again by their own activity if they would but engage themselves, believing that they would most certainly perish if they were to neglect to do so."[16] It is out of their spiritual immaturity and fear of their condition that they push back on themselves and their own self-effort rather than drawing near to God to abide in him.

Notice that each of these figures considers both experience and the nature of developmental maturation in the spiritual life. This kind of teaching was standard in the Protestant tradition. This conversation also had an eye on the psychological development and health of a person, recognizing how various "dispositions" and "tempers" change how one experiences the life of faith. Perhaps most obviously, the "disease of melancholy"—what we might think of as depression—was a major factor in how they understood this. In talking about spiritual deadness, for instance, à Brakel writes, "Someone who has a melancholy and despondent disposition will also be very vulnerable to spiritual deadness."[17] Richard Baxter famously has a section in his book *The Christian Directory* that focuses on melancholy. He talks about what we would call both nature and nurture, giving thirty-nine points about the "melancholic person."

We are not the first people to think about the psychological realities of human life and the various ways our bodies and souls relate. The entire Christian tradition talks about these things and focuses on what maturing a soul looks like. But unlike our contemporary conversation, they would often note how Satan works to exacerbate these issues and how he uses them against us in our life with God. Martin Luther, for instance, writes about how Satan confuses the mind to make us think that the only thing Christ ever offers is consolation. When we experience terror, Satan tries to lead us to believe that we do not have Christ, seeking to undo us with despair.[18] The traditional psychology of the Christian was as much about spiritual maturation as it was about spiritual warfare.

Consistently, our own Protestant tradition worries that we turn to ourselves rather than to God when we struggle with desolation, and the pastor-theologians in our tradition continually point to the weakness of the flesh and the work of Satan to exploit and confuse the Christian. Puritan Richard Sibbes (1577–1635) considers the question of why God would lead us in this way and argues that Christ lets us see the necessity of our dependence upon him by leaving us to ourselves. The goal is knowing the source of our Christian existence is outside of ourselves.[19] Similarly, meditating on Colossians 3:3, "Your life is hidden with Christ in God,"

Sibbes narrates how the Christian life "is a hidden life." He goes on to reveal our temptation to live by our senses rather than by faith, where we trust what our senses tell us rather than the fact that our true life is hidden with Christ in God. He claims, "God will have it so that this life shall be now hid, that we may live by the promises, though we have no feeling at all; that we may persuade ourselves in the greatest desertions and extremities, yet I have a hidden life in Christ."[20]

While our conversation partners for this path have been from the Reformed tradition, it would be wrongheaded to assume that the broader Protestant tradition doesn't include these themes. John Wesley, for instance, writes, "Whether he gives us joy or sorrow of heart, whether he inspires us with vigour and cheerfulness, or permits us to sink into numbness of soul, into dryness and heaviness, 'tis all with the same view, viz., to restore us to health, to liberty, to holiness."[21] Wesley recognized that the Lord prods us with different kinds of experiences but does so because of what spiritual formation actually is. It is about life with the Father in Christ by the Spirit. All that God leads us into, Wesley argues, "mild or severe, point at no other end than this." What is this end? Our sanctification: "They are all designed either to wean us from what is not, or to unite us to what is worthy [of] our affection."[22]

For the Protestant tradition broadly, desertions teach us to see the ways we long not for faith but for sight. The desert seasons and desolation unveil the truth of the heart and what needs purifying by God's holy presence and love. By referring to the senses, Sibbes highlights that sight is only one of the ways we seek to find security in our lives with Christ, grounded in our own experience. We want to be able to look at our experience to tell us we've done it. We're okay. We've arrived. But Christ calls us to faith. In desertion we only have faith. In desertion we have to trust not in our experiences but in Christ's steadfast love and faithfulness.

Even beyond these more ancient sources, Charles Spurgeon (1834–1892) understood the theme of the dark night well. He proclaims,

> Now there are many who have rejoiced in the presence of God for a season; they have basked in the sunshine God has been pleased to give them in the earlier stages of their Christian career; they have walked along the "green pastures," by the side of the "still waters," and suddenly—in a month or two—they find that glorious sky is clouded: instead of "green pastures," they have to tread the sandy desert; in the place of "still waters," they find streams brackish to their taste and bitter to their spirits, and they say, "Surely, if I were a child of God this would not happen." Oh! say not so, thou who art walking in darkness. The best of God's saints have their nights; the dearest of his children have to walk through a weary wilderness. There is not a Christian who has enjoyed perpetual happiness, there is no believer who can always sing a song of joy. It is not every lark that can always carol. It is not every star that can always be seen. And not every Christian is always happy. Perhaps the King of Saints gave you a season of great joy at first because you were a raw recruit and he would not put you into the roughest part of the battle when you had first enlisted. You were a tender plant, and he nursed you in the hot-house till you could stand severe weather. You were a young child, and therefore he wrapped you in furs and clothed you in the softest mantle. But now you have become strong and the case is different.[23]

The Protestant tradition has always wrestled with consolation, the desert, and desolation. This is just a brief glimpse into some of these figures, including Jonathan Edwards, whose experiences we have already narrated briefly in this book. The Protestant tradition not only spoke deeply about these seasons, but they often lamented about how few understood them. This is particularly disconcerting since even fewer seem to understand these things today.

If we are going to navigate our own lives with the Lord, and certainly if we are going to shepherd others, we need to understand what Scripture and our own tradition help us see. It turns out that *our God is a withdrawing God*, not in reality but in experience. But he is a God who does so in and for love. This is the continual witness of Scripture, and this is exactly what we see throughout the Christian tradition as a whole and the Protestant tradition more narrowly.

Path 2:
The Church in Despair

In this second path, we want to briefly consider our experiences in the church. While experiences with the church differ from person to person, everything we have said about the Christian life for individuals can be said corporately about churches as well. Churches go through seasons of consolation, the desert, and desolation. A church, as a body of Christ in a given location, is called to mature together in the faith (to grow up in Christ to "mature manhood" [Eph. 4:13]). This means that churches are called to wrestle through the dryness and dust of the desert seasons and to discern what the Lord is calling them to be purified of (to "put off") and what the Lord is calling them to do (to "put on").

After several years lamenting what the churches of our youth didn't provide for us, we were able to see that they did provide some very important things. In our spiritual infancies, we were nurtured in the faith and given a lot of immediate opportunities to get involved. It was clear that Jesus required that we give every aspect of our life to him, and the church was a central part of our lives. This was a profound gift. But these same churches had bought into a vision of the Christian life that had everything to do with either exciting the will (Kyle's experience) or inflating the mind with information (John's experience), and neither addressed the temptation of moralism and fixing of the self that was actually taking over our lives.

When churches are in the desert and in desolation, it is first felt by those serving in leadership. There is a weight that seems to sit on things, when prior ministry felt light and free. In our experience, when our leaders felt the burden of the congregation, instead of shepherding us into and through our struggles with the Lord, they would cast a new vision, start a new ministry, or hire a well-known person to give the congregation an adrenaline shot of consolation. They were digging deeper into what they had always been doing, thinking they just needed to do it with renewed energy. When it seemed to work, they were celebrated as great leaders. What no one seemed to notice was that Christians either left the church or remained with increasing confusion, isolation, and despair.

One of the most deceptive realities of pumping up the will for individuals or giving an adrenaline shot to the church is that it seems to work in the short term. I (Kyle) remember getting a new worship leader in a church that was struggling with boredom. It reinvigorated the church for a bit. Likewise, when we hired a new teaching pastor whose insights grabbed our minds, it made us feel like things were working again, but only for a while. In the short term, the new vision to "change the world" captivated our imaginations. But after this initial corporate passion wore off, the same struggles kept emerging. Soon, the pastor's new vision made us bitter. *Yeah right, I've heard this before.* Now, the pastor's insights were missed because I just spaced out during his sermons. The constant prodding to get more involved or bring my friends felt manipulative rather than missional. I felt like I was being harnessed rather than shepherded.

Increasingly, there was an ever-widening gap between what I felt I should be and what was really true of me. Over time, my spiritual life began to feel like the hard fall after a sugar high, and continually pumping up my will to praise God felt forced and deceptive. My obedience and spiritual life felt as dry as dust. I tried sparking passion in my soul over and over, hoping it would catch my life on fire, but it left me numb. What no one said, but I learned implicitly, was that I shouldn't put words to the truth of my heart, and I needed instead to keep on singing revival songs until it worked.

The longer I was there, the more I felt the tension between what was true and what was fantasy. It was true that the church was growing numerically, and we talked about that all the time. But it was also true that there was a stream of people leaving out the back door, bewildered and angry. We didn't talk about that. In fact, it was the people who had been Christians the longest, and often been at the church the longest, who left to find something else. Some of them, no doubt, went looking for consolation elsewhere. But many of them were bored because they were growing into their adolescence in the faith and were still being treated like they were in kindergarten.

We have seen that in Paul's pastoral ministry he was able to discern between those who needed milk and those who were ready for solid food. He assumed that some people were infants in Christ, some were adolescents in the faith, and others were adults. Paul had a developmental spirituality that helped him pastor in wisdom. This has been lost or at least obscured. A key reason why the church has struggled with maturation in recent memory is because the church does not think developmentally. When we don't have a sense of the developmental progress of a Christian, we cannot preach to specific Christian experiences. When we don't have a sense of how people grow, we will give steak to infants and milk to adults. We forget that our job is not to generate consolation but to walk in the Spirit. But we do need guides. We do need shepherds. But we need shepherds who have taken this journey before.

Instead of understanding Christian growth developmentally, the church has unknowingly equated spiritual formation with natural formation. We assume that as long as you show up, are committed, and work hard, then you will grow spiritually as you grow in age. I have often heard people refer to others in the church as "wise" and "mature" simply because they have been around a long time. In this sense we often assume that we can use worldly metrics to discern success rather than the fruit of the Spirit. What the church needs to have is a vision of God's work to mature a soul throughout a life and a vision for how the people of God can engage each other throughout that process of maturation.

In our teaching, preaching, and communities, we need to have a sense of how the Lord works and what it means to encourage one another in life with Christ. If we don't, we will inevitably be churches of adult people who are infants in Christ, or at best, adolescents who are continually struggling with the spiritual equivalent of puberty. But perhaps even more so, we have to wrestle together with what it means to lead, minister, guide, and care for each other in seasons of desolation. The deep belief that we can generate consolation, or that we should seek to do so, inoculates us against the work of God to call us to himself. This is why we have to resist the temptation to simply generate moralism or an experience of consolation and ignore the truth of what is really going on.

So what does this mean in practice? For a worship leader, you have to realize that much of your congregation may be in consolation, or they may be in desolation. You can trust that there are people trying to use worship to silence their conscience or to pump up their will instead of coming to God in the truth. Simply naming or framing the reality of what people might be experiencing is a way to locate them in the truth and to help them navigate singing a praise song when they are really despairing. Shepherd them to the Lord in light of what may be going on in every season of the soul.

Similarly, in preaching, we have to remember that we are not simply passing on information or motivating people to obey in their own power. The goal isn't to help your people get a good score on a theology or Bible exam. You are shepherding your people in the presence of the Lord in light of his Word. So when you proclaim his Word, you need to name ways that people might hear it in the flesh or the ways they might hear it differently in early consolation, the desert, or desolation. You need to know that they are hearing his Word and their consciences, and when the "thoughts" emerge (Rom. 2:14–15), they are having to navigate a confusing experience. Naming these things does not take long but is significant in calling people out of hiding and covering to come to Jesus.

In short, in various ways, we need to corporately ask the Lord, *What does it mean to be faithful to you here?* We are tempted, instead, to try to awaken passion to make us feel like we are doing something meaningful. We are tempted to walk by our senses rather than by faith. So we need to ask: What might it look like to corporately hold open before the Lord our temptations as a people, and even our failures, trusting in the presence of the purifying fire of love?

For both church leaders and church attendees, perhaps one of the more pressing questions we need to ask is this: Are we captivated by Jesus and embracing the truth of his kingdom reign, or do we need to sensationalize the dangers around us, focusing more on the enemies outside our walls to caffeinate our wills with fear to generate obedience? Maybe instead of focusing on enemies, we simply use guilt to get people to act in the ways we want rather than pointing them to Christ. There are nefarious enemies of the Christian, to be sure, and we are guilty, but the end of those things is Christ and not advancing our own personal ministerial agenda. Confronted with what feels like dead and lifeless wills in our people, too many turn to techniques of the flesh to wake them up rather than reframing the whole of their lives according to the gospel.

While many might relate to our experiences, there is also a newer experience we are seeing in the church. In some churches, a leader learns about spiritual formation and decides to take the church in a new direction. At first, there is a lot of excitement. People who have begun to experience the desert see this as a new avenue to find the rivers of living water they so desperately long for. They hear exciting teaching about spiritual practices, community, and discipleship, and they buy in. Then, a couple of years later, everything feels like it's falling apart. What happened?

When people grab on to a vision of spiritual practices there is a tendency to think these practices will fix our problems. That they will make life work again. They will provide the growth we're looking for. In the short term, there is some hope that it's working. Anything new seems to fill us with the excitement of possibility and hope, but before long, these practices begin to waken the deep things of the heart. Vices in the character are increasingly exposed, and spiritual practices no longer feel life-giving. In fact, they feel bad because we are seeing the lack of love in our hearts. It feels like things are going backwards. Increasingly, all this talk about spiritual discipline feels legalistic. It is here where we need to call people out of hiding and send them to the Lord.

What few talk about but everyone experiences is that much of what goes on in the church is interpreted on the level of *feeling*. When a congregant says, "This *feels* legalistic," they are not making a theological judgment but are talking about their subconscious theology that guides their lives. If we respond, "Well, it isn't legalistic," we are not actually helping them. When people begin practicing things like silence, solitude, vulnerable community, and other spiritual practices the evangelical church has always practiced, *we should expect that the deep sins, pains, and brokenness of their hearts will be unveiled.* In other words, people will start spinning, and it will feel to them like they are spinning away from growth and into despair. They need someone to shepherd them through these realities and not merely prescribe more spiritual disciplines.

When folks start feeling like things are not working, there is a tendency to urge people to continue on the path, but the only category people have for this experience is that it *feels* like legalism, or it *feels* like being abandoned. In the first sense, when folks talk about the feeling of legalism, they are beginning to recognize that they are not using these spiritual practices to offer themselves to the Lord. They are probably doing these things legalistically, thinking that if they just do them, they will create Christian growth and joy. It is not helpful to tell them to stop feeling that way, or worse, to just assert that it isn't legalistic. The whole point of spiritual practices is that they mimic the experience of the desert by following the Lord in difficulty and often trial to reveal what is in our hearts. The Lord is showing them the idolatry of their hearts and inviting them to abide in him and seek him in these places, and yet it feels like he is absent. Confronted with this confusion, people just leave and go elsewhere, hoping to find the consolation that will make them feel like they are doing things right again.

The church must embrace a developmental spirituality, shepherding people to walk by faith and not by sight, and not just push people into spiritual practices. Sending people off into practices like silence and solitude without the proper spiritual care will only be disorienting. Most will go into silence expecting to have a profound experience of the Lord. What more often happens is that they have a profoundly confusing experience of *themselves*. Many—perhaps most—will assume that everyone else is having a different experience, or they will assume they are just doing it wrong. Some in this state will begin to wonder if they are saved at all, which has always been the worry about desolation in the Protestant tradition (see path 1). Much damage has been done by pushing people into practice instead of shepherding them to their Lord.

Our hope is that this book, and our previous book, *Where Prayer Becomes Real*, will help shepherd folks into the reality of these experiences. We both found something much deeper than we ever knew in our early consolation when we discovered that the Lord wanted us to draw near in the truth. Pastors are needed who have walked this path and can shepherd others in it. This is what "Path 1: Why Have I Never Heard This Before?" revealed from the Protestant tradition, and also what "Path 3: A Call for Spiritual Theology" offers some resources for. But beyond resources, for someone to pastor others well in this, they will have to navigate the desert and desolation while in leadership (a profoundly disorienting dynamic). For this, see "Path 4: To Those in Ministry."

Path 3:
A Call for Spiritual Theology

A question may be emerging within you that goes something like this: *The message of this book really resonates with me. Is this something I'm called to?* Maybe you've been reading Christian books for years, and you are interested in thinking deeply about the Christian life, the Bible, and theology, but you haven't seen someone engage the more existential questions of life with God. If you have read path 1, you see that this is not a new discussion. Raising questions about our lived experience has always been central to evangelical thought and practice. This is not the place to talk about why this fell out of the seminary curriculum, and subsequently the church, but it is worth pausing here to consider what spiritual theology is and what the calling of spiritual theology entails.

When I (Kyle) decided to study Jonathan Edwards for my PhD, the reason was because Edwards was among the final wave of thinkers to thoroughly integrate their theology and spirituality. After Edwards, theologians often talked about doctrine as abstracted from life with God in and through the Spirit (although there are important counterexamples). Spirituality began to emerge as a field of its own, divorced from our theological beliefs. When this happened, both disciplines died. Theology often digresses into a discipline that seeks knowledge apart from the presence of God—a knowledge that puffs up—and spirituality becomes unmoored from its theological roots, leaving it worldly and broken. We desperately need a reintegration of these two, focusing on the lived reality of the Christian life.

When John and I wrote our book *Where Prayer Becomes Real*, the precursor to this book, we wanted to approach it as spiritual theologians. This led us to give a distinctively *Christian* account of prayer, showing how gospel-shaped prayer leads us to the Father in and through the intercession of the Son and Spirit for us, through us, and from within us. But while that is important, it is not enough. We need more than a theoretical description of prayer; we also need practical guidance. A good book on prayer needs to tell you what a distinctively Christian vision of prayer is, but it should also give you practical wisdom about the act of prayer. Sadly, it is rare to find these two things balanced, but even if they were, that would not be enough.

I have read many books on prayer. Many I've read were helpful, but most choose between being either theoretically insightful or practically helpful. But we were convinced that a third thing is needed. A good book on prayer needs to explain what is happening in prayer itself: What is the Spirit doing here? Why does my mind wander? How do I navigate my negative experiences of prayer? Why does my heart condemn me, at times, when I draw near to God (1 John 3:19–20), and why do I assume that God is the one condemning me? Notice that spiritual theology is going to address the lived reality of life with God, and that means our actual life with God must be brought into our theology. We sought to integrate the theoretical and practical with the lived reality of life with Jesus because each of these are central features for what spiritual theology requires.

This means that when we're doing spiritual theology, we want to attend carefully to what Scripture says about sanctification, growth, and maturation. We want to understand the content of our faith, attending to what it means to be in Christ and filled with the Spirit. But then we also need to consider our sin and brokenness. So we need to attend to what anger is in general but also *what our personal anger is about*. We need to unfold our worry and consider what is going on in our souls as well as others so that we can help shepherd God's people to him.

Put differently, a spiritual theologian is going to go beyond an abstract description to address how this really works in life. Not only do we want to know *that* the Bible says to put off anger, but we want to wrestle through what it looks like for someone to actually put off anger. We want to consider the temptations in seeking to be faithful and the ways that our sin, brokenness, pain, and rebellion undermine God's maturation of us. There is a great temptation in the church and academy to just assert biblical imperatives ("Put off anger!") and imagine that if we just get excited and shout it into our souls, it will happen.

Ultimately, spiritual theologians are interested in understanding what it means to retrain our lives in the Holy Spirit. This means we will have to attend to the nature, processes, and directives for life in the Spirit by faith. This means we will have to walk into spiritual maturation ourselves because this task is not simply an academic one but requires our whole lives. For folks like John and me, who teach in both the academy and the church, this calling requires years of studying the Bible, church history, theology, and philosophy, as well as considering ancient and modern descriptions of personhood, psychology, and growth. But that isn't true for everyone. Many of our students, for instance, study with us because they want to grow spiritually and they want to walk alongside others in that process. For them, seminary is as much a hospital as it is a training ground for the care of souls.

Spiritual theology is about living life before the face of God as we offer ourselves to him in Christ as living sacrifices. This is walking in and by the Spirit of holiness and love as we seek holiness and love from him and for him. Ultimately, God is the one who gives us wisdom, so this is not a mere academic endeavor but a personal submission to the Lord. With God in heart and Scripture in hand, the spiritual theologian goes into the church and seeks to understand two things. First, how does the Holy Spirit transform individually? In other words, how does he actually work in individual lives? And second, how does the Holy Spirit transform corporately? How does he actually shape us together in Christ, who is our head, with a growth that comes from God (Col. 2:19)? This is what our classes are about, and we are humbled to get to do this task.

What this means is that spiritual theology really is *pastoral* theology—theology for the sake of shepherding others to Christ in and by the Spirit. If you are going to work with people, you are going to have to engage in pastoral theology because you are going to have to ask the question, How does this work? Spiritual theology is unavoidable for anyone who is seeking to be faithful to Scripture and consider what it actually means to love their neighbor as themselves, to put off anger, and so on. You can't escape those questions if you want to grow and help others grow. If you believe you are called to minister to others—in a full-time "paid ministry" role or just in your life ministry—it could be that a degree in spiritual theology is what you are called to give yourself to.

John and I help to lead an institute in spiritual formation that addresses the communal and formative dynamics of life with Christ. We have reimagined the seminary curriculum around these dynamics, seeking to maintain what the seminary has always done well and combine that with spiritual formation in a cohort of people all wrestling through what a deeper life with God entails.

For more information on the programs we offer, see https://www.biola.edu/talbot/academics/isf.

For more information on our new church-based spiritual formation initiative called "The Journey," see https://www.learn.biola.edu/bundles/the-journey-phase-1.

Path 4:
To Those in Ministry

Many reading this book will struggle with the call to abide amid the Lord's confusing work. It is a hard call, even though it is the call of love. But for those in vocational ministry—pastors, missionaries, ministry leaders—the call is even more difficult. For many of these folks, the weight of ministry expectations can be debilitating. Many of us struggle to be honest about the truth of our hearts, but that becomes even more difficult when you think it is your job to be "beyond these things."

Many people come to seminary in consolation, or they start ministry in consolation, and that bolsters them for several years. Once the regular rhythms of ministry are established, they find themselves in the desert, faithfully grinding away and trusting that the Lord is at work. But this is a particularly lonely place. What often ends up fueling this season is the fact that people are being blessed. The visible fruit of ministry often helps to buoy against feeling too "tossed by the waves" (assuming there is visible fruit), but in desolation even this begins to feel like dust and straw.

John and I have both walked through desolation in ministry. We have taught content that seemed dead and lifeless and watched it enliven and awaken souls to the truths of God.

We have preached and watched the people of God drink the rivers of living water when our own souls felt parched and withered. Sometimes this was profoundly confusing and led us into seasons in which we were tempted to despair. What made the most significant difference later on, however, was walking through these seasons in contexts where we could go to someone and open our hearts to them, trusting that we could be heard, seen, known, and supported. For many, that isn't the case.

It is hard to fully appreciate the difficulty of a pastor who doesn't think the elder board would understand or provide support in desolation. It is hard to fathom how difficult it is for a missionary in the desert or in desolation who sends out fundraising letters and does not believe being honest will help support their mission. Leaders often bear the weight of their spiritual life in a way that leads them away from the truth because they have internalized the idea that they need to at least *look* like they have it all figured out or their ministry will come crashing down. The weight of leadership often stifles one's honesty because it feels too difficult to name the truth and keep going, especially with the possible criticism and misunderstanding that may follow.

The struggle for anyone in full-time ministry is recognizing that the Lord is teaching what he always does—that his power is made perfect in their weakness. The seasons of consolation don't often teach us this truth. The confusion of the desert and desolation reveals that God's work does not depend on our savvy or sophistication. As with Moses, who was willing to serve but knew he couldn't speak well, the Lord is showing us that he is calling us into weakness to reveal his power. The Lord is teaching us to abide and to trust. And as always, the Lord is showing us what is in our hearts.

What we will discover in these seasons is that our ministry activity is fueled by a lot of different things. For most, I would assume, there is real faith, hope, and love establishing their ministry, but it is often wound tightly together with things like pride, grandiosity, and envy. But there is often a lot of guilt, shame, and anxiety in the background as well. Alternatively, others might notice that they have fueled their devotion from their goodness, like the older brother in the parable of the Father with two sons.

Too many worry that their ministry depends on them being strong, good, and sophisticated, and this shuts them off to honesty. When the Lord shows them what is in their hearts, they end up feeling like they are failing. In these places, the Lord's invitation into his strength feels like losing everything, and so they are unable to hear the gracious call of the Lord: "Unless a grain of wheat falls into the earth and dies, it remains alone; but if it dies, it bears much fruit" (John 12:24). Instead of laying down their lives in these moments, they remain alone, and too often ministry feels like a lonely path of trying hard to generate faithfulness.

The first call in this season is honesty with God. In our book *Where Prayer Becomes Real*, we offer something of a course on drawing near to God in the truth. We encourage you to commit to honestly wrestling with the Lord in this season and seeking him in the midst of your struggle in ministry. But this also means you will have to cultivate a certain watchfulness of heart. What does your ministry awaken in your heart? What sorts of struggles emerge as you minister? What are your fears, anxieties, and worries, and where do you turn to deal with them instead of bringing them to the Lord? For many, the only time these struggles show up in prayer is in asking the Lord to make them go away. Instead, be open to the truth of your heart and present yourself to

God. This can feel like a very lonely time. Allow the Lord to take you on a journey of your heart where you can find his mercy, kindness, and love where you really need it.

For those in ministry, perhaps more than most, it will be important to pay attention to envy in these seasons. Is there someone else's ministry you envy? Is there another church, ministry, or pastor you look at and find yourself coveting or demeaning? Envy often makes us think things like *Their success will actually be bad for them. It would be better if I had success since I would be able to handle it better.*[24] In these seasons, it may be helpful to recall Jesus's rebuke to Peter for focusing on John rather than the Lord's specific calling for him: "What is that to you? You follow me!" (John 21:22).

We might need to hear:

- ❖ What is it to you if that person's ministry thrives and yours seems to wither?
- ❖ What is it to you if I make them famous and I call you into obscurity?
- ❖ What is it to you if I have called them into places of influence?

Seek Jesus in the truth and entrust yourself and your ministry to him.

To walk this path well inevitably requires that you walk alongside others. So, right after embracing honesty in prayer as the first step, the second step is to start a conversation about the ways you struggle. As we share with churches and ministries around the country (and even, at times, the world) the ways we have personally struggled in ministry, we have both found that when we name our temptations, struggles, and failures, people immediately start sharing.

People understand the difficulties of the desert and desolation if they are shown what they are, and they are often desperate for guidance. Find people who can walk this path with you. Be open to the possibility that he is taking you into this season because he is about to take your people and your ministry into places that need a shepherd who has walked this path before them.

Journeying with the Lord in ministry can be difficult, and many have found it easier to just stop journeying with him. It proves easier to just focus on doing good work. The Lord calls us to more. Pause and consider with him what it would look like to present yourself to him in the truth, and trust that he is enough for you. *Lord, my life is hidden with you in God* (Col. 3:3). *You are my life. You are my hope. You are faithful. Lord, here I am. I want you, and I want to abide in you. Show me all the ways I don't abide in you and instead seek other ways to try to generate an obedience of the flesh. Lord, lead me to yourself to bear much fruit.*

Path 5:

Going Forward in Faith

Our hope for this final path is to orient you to your Lord in the midst of a confusing and disorienting season. This is not the time to start questioning your faith or looking to your experiences for an answer as to what is going on. This is not a season to try to pump up your will with excitement and passion. This is a time to seek the Lord in the truth. Left to our own presuppositions, we often do all kinds of odd things in these seasons, especially in our prayer lives. We want to provide some steadying pastoral wisdom for how to navigate life with the Lord during these times.

Initially, when you find yourself in the desert, you'll often notice it first in your spiritual life. Maybe your mind is wandering in prayer or in reading the Word, or you find your spiritual life is dry as dust and you wonder where God is. Do not be silent in this, but tell God everything you are feeling. You might pray through lament psalms like Psalm 77 or 88 and cry out to God with exactly what you are feeling. I (John) recall going through this time, and rather than telling God how I was feeling in prayer, I would press the pause button on my prayer life (as if there is such a button!) and give myself a pep talk on being a better Christian. I would try to pump myself up by turning against myself, demanding to know why my life was so dry, why I was bored in prayer, and how I needed to have more passion. Once buoyed by my self-talk, I would then unpause prayer and start talking to God again.

Notice, however, I wasn't really *with* God in any of this. I was, first, just talking to myself and then just talking *at* him. I didn't think he could handle the truth (see our previous book, *Where Prayer Becomes Real*, for more on this). What I failed to really sit with was that God was right there with me when I was talking to myself rather than talking with him. It never dawned on me to share with him exactly how I was feeling. I didn't think God wanted to hear it, and I even wondered whether he could hear this part of my soul. Once I began to share all my feelings with God, it brought me to a new depth of being with him in truth in his love and forgiveness. So do not be silent. Utilize the psalms of lament and bring your complaints and struggles to God through them. Trust that the psalms show you what kind of God he is by showing you what he can hear.

Second, when we are wandering in seasons of the desert and desolation, the temptation is to feel guilty for this dryness and to focus on what is wrong with our life. Our flesh believes that if we are doing it right—that if we are praying with fervency and reading the Word with affection—all will be well again. The question is not, first and foremost, how we got where we are but what it is that God is doing there. The desert and desolation are works of God. It is true, of course, that these seasons would not exist if we were not sinful. We won't have this experience in eternity. But now God has decided to lead you into a season to show you what is true of your sin and brokenness. God is using this season to show us ourselves in the context of his truth, love, and forgiveness. Our calling here is to track what the Spirit is doing in these times and cooperate with him.

Third, when we are in the desert and desolation, spiritual practices will be different. Specifically, their purpose will change. During early consolation, things like praying, reading the Word, and performing acts of service bind the young believer's heart and life to the Lord despite the sins and vices in the soul. In early consolation our spiritual lives mirror God's goodness and grace alone. But in seasons of the desert and desolation, spiritual practices no longer encourage but rather *mirror* what is in the hidden places of our hearts. This is why it is so confusing. Spiritual practices become little mirrors of the deep places in us that don't care about God, prayer, or others.

The change in our spiritual practices explains why we often only recognize the desert and desolation in our devotion or ministries and maybe most in prayer (or our lack of prayer, if we stop praying). When we pray in the desert or desolation, our minds wander to their real treasures, and we imagine we are failing (see Matt. 6:21). But this is an invitation to be known and not merely to be good. When we are reading the Word and are secretly bored, our flesh tells us that we aren't trying hard enough. But this is God calling us to himself in the truth. This comes as a great surprise to us, particularly after times of consolation. But now the Lord wants to show us hidden parts of our heart that do not love him, that are full of selfish desires and idols. This is not a time to hide or muster up energy and passion but is a time to look into the mirror of reality with Jesus and tell him all. Open to the truth of what is in your soul—holding open these disordered desires and broken parts of ourselves—and share them with God. He is greater than your heart and already knows all (1 John 3:19–20), and he wants you to share with him.

Fourth, these seasons of desert and desolation are intended to teach us that we cannot fix ourselves, that only God can form Christ within us, and that apart from him we can do nothing (John 15:5). This is a time to let go of our need to silence the feelings of guilt and shame by working harder and instead to see them as invitations to fly to Christ for love and forgiveness. Do not be afraid of your guilt, shame, and sin, and do not seek to manage them in your own power. Come to Christ. Because of Christ's work, these are now opportunities to abide.

Fifth, as you travel through these seasons of desert and desolation, resist the temptation to generate consolation. Remember that God's mercies really are new every morning, and they are ready for us—whether in consolation or desolation. It is not your job to generate anything. Your calling is to be open to God in obedience and abide in him in whatever you are experiencing. In some ways, the simplest thing to do when confronted by moralism and the desire to perfect yourself in the flesh is to open your heart to him and tell him. This is where we can find freedom from the need to generate consolation and feel good about our spiritual lives—by opening our hearts to what Christ is doing in our soul through the Spirit.

Sixth, the desert and desolation are seasons in which you need a mentor or pastoral guide who can assist you in navigating them. You need someone to mirror back to you what happens when you desire to fix your life by just praying harder, mustering passion, or trying to generate consolation in worship. You need someone who can help you understand why you desire to pray less and obey less when the feeling of consolation does not return. Now you need a mentor who knows something of life in the Spirit through all the various seasons of the soul to assist you in opening your heart in truth to God, who sees all and is praying for you (see Rom. 8:26–29). This mentor can assist you in opening to God in your neediness and sin and help you maintain a Godward vision, always going to Christ for help. This is one of the purposes of the body of Christ in assisting souls for life in the Spirit.

Finally, the seasons of the desert and desolation are times in God's sovereignty when he is doing a unique work to call you to himself. This is an invitation to take a journey through the soul into the very presence of the One who lives within us and is transforming our hearts to conform to his own. These are times to let the Lord search our heart (Ps. 139:23–24) and to open all our expectations and anger and hopes—whatever is in the soul—to him. This is similar to Paul's call when the Lord gifted him with a thorn in the flesh into weakness and dependence upon God (2 Cor. 12:7–10). These are times to know God deeply in the truth of your own sins, letting Jesus teach you about them, so that you can take his yoke and lay down your own. These are seasons to know that he is gentle and humble in heart, and he is the One who can give rest to our souls (Matt. 11:28–30).

ACKNOWLEDGMENTS

We would like to thank Talbot School of Theology and Biola University for the support. In particular, the Institute for Spiritual Formation has been such a profound context in which to teach, write, and relate with students and colleagues. Each of you has been such a profound gift to us. Praying with you and walking through life with the Lord together is a journey we didn't know was possible when we first had the dream to go into academic work. Being with you all has been an absolute joy for us.

Our colleagues at the Institute for Spiritual Formation, in particular, have been such a profound gift to us. Judy TenElshof, Betsy Barber, Steve Porter, Berry Bishop, Dave Merrill, Megen Phillips, Chris Baker, Ellen Balzun, and Donna Ostrom, several of whom have now been ministering in different contexts, have challenged us and been wonderful companions on this journey of faith. Thank you all for your kindness, support, and encouragement.

There have been many other folks who have helped support and encourage us along the way whom we would like to mention specifically. Jody and Jeanie Humber for their encouragement and support of our work. You both have been used by God in incredible ways to bless us, and we are grateful for you. Thank you as well to Austin and Sarah Green. Your encouragement and support have been a blessing. Austin Green, Brooks Montgomery, Matthew Jordan, and Jamin Goggin all provided helpful feedback on the manuscript, and we are thankful for their willingness to help us. Likewise, Kyle's mother Leslie, sister Alison, and wife Kelli gave profoundly helpful feedback in earlier and later phases of the manuscript, and the book is much better for that.

I (Kyle) would like to thank Jamin Goggin, Ryan Peterson, and Tim Pickavance, whose friendship, encouragement, and support have been a true gift of the Lord. To Redeemer Church, the ecclesial context in which I work, I see it as a real privilege of my life to serve and minister with you all. I have served as an elder at Redeemer while working on this project, and much of this book is a vision for what I hope we can be: a church that walks with people through every developmental stage of the Christian faith. To the elders I served with, I'm thankful for each of you and how you all embody so profoundly what it means to serve in love. Likewise, to Dominic Vincent, Robbie Goforth, and John Poston, former elders who helped pastor me when I need them most. Bless you, my friends.

Finally, to my wife Kelli, for her support, encouragement, and love. You are such a gift to me, and I am so grateful for you. I'm thankful that I get to walk this journey of faith with you. To my daughter Brighton and son Oliver, you both fill me with such joy. I absolutely love being your dad. Brighton, may the Lord teach you, in each phase of your life with him, what it means to draw near to him and rest in his love. Oliver, may the Lord open your heart to his grace, mercy, and forgiveness, and may you know the love of God that surpasses understanding. My precious family, may the Lord continue to bind our hearts together in love, and lead us in his way.

I (John) would like to thank my wife Greta for her spiritual friendship these fifty years. She helped bring me to the Lord in high school and has been my spiritual partner, joy, and confidant in all seasons of consolation, the desert, and desolation in our fifty years together. Bless you. You are so dear and deep in my heart. My thanks also to my mentors of old, some of whom are now gone to the Lord: Drs. Robert Saucy, John Finch, and Bruce Narramore. Bless you for how the Lord worked in your lives and how you impacted my life in Christ and in the Spirit. Each of you was used to open my life to the Spirit. You also are so dear in my heart.

Special thanks go to all the people who assisted in the production of this volume. Our fearless agent Jenni Burke and all of the folks at Illuminate Literary Agency have been so encouraging and helpful to us. Thank you for your support of us in general and this project specifically. Thank you to the good folks at Baker Books, especially Brian and Eddie, and all the folks in marketing, design, and editing. It has been great to work with all of you. Thank you all for your excitement about this project and your continued support.

NOTES

Chapter 3 Wading into the Unknown

1. Our own approach to consolation and desolation has been impacted by many different figures. When John first started wrestling through these things, he was introduced to John of the Cross and Bernard of Clairvaux, both of whom offered developmental theories of the Christian life. Kyle was impacted by similar material in the Puritan and evangelical spiritual traditions, often through the language of consolation and spiritual desertion, which we narrate in path 1 at the end of this book. For some of John's early work on this, see "Musings on the Dark Night of the Soul: Insights from St. John of the Cross on a Developmental Spirituality," in *The Journal of Psychology and Theology* 28, no. 4 (2000): 293–307.

2. *The Complete Works of Richard Sibbes*, ed. Alexander Balloch Grosart, vol. 5 (James Nichol, 1863), 84.

Chapter 4 Avoiding God in Our Passion

1. Kyle gives an overview of Jonathan Edwards's view of spiritual formation in his book *Formed for the Glory of God: Learning from the Spiritual Practices of Jonathan Edwards* (IVP, 2013).

2. *The Works of Jonathan Edwards*, ed. George S. Claghorn, vol. 16, *Letters and Personal Writings* (Yale University Press, 1998), 795.

3. *Works of Jonathan Edwards*, 16:795.

4. *Works of Jonathan Edwards*, 16:799.

5. *Works of Jonathan Edwards*, 16:803.

6. *Works of Jonathan Edwards*, 16:803.

7. This point is made by Edwards in the final sign of his "positive signs" of religious affection. For an overview, read my chapter, "Jonathan

Edwards' *A Treatise Concerning Religious Affections*" in *The Oxford Handbook of Reformed Theology*, ed. Michael Allen and Scott Swain (Oxford, 2020), 295–311.

Chapter 5 Avoiding God in Our Brokenness

1. Author and professor of psychology S. Bruce Narramore addresses some of the psychological dynamics of guilt and shame as they played out in Adam and Eve. Importantly, however, it is necessary to have an account of guilt that isn't seen as bad, because it recognizes the truth that we are guilty. The problem is not that we *feel* guilty; it is that we *are* guilty. Narramore helps narrate guilt and shame well experientially but misses the important value of guilt in bringing us to the Lord who secures our salvation in himself. *No Condemnation: Rethinking Guilt Motivation in Counseling, Preaching, and Parenting* (Wipf & Stock, 1984), 26–34; 57–65.

Interlude Losing Grip on the Gospel

1. Martin Luther, "A Brief Instruction on What to Look For and Expect in the Gospels," in *Martin Luther's Basic Theological Writings* (Fortress Press, 2012), 72.

Chapter 6 Avoiding God in Our Goodness

1. Herman Bavinck is characteristically helpful on this point. When comparing the spiritual life with the moral life, he writes, "There is, however, a life other than the moral one: a spiritual life." Unsurprisingly, he immediately turns to Galatians 2:20, as do we, to highlight the more profound nature of life in Christ. *Reformed Ethics*, ed. John Bolt, vol. 1, *Created, Fallen, and Converted Humanity* (Baker Academic, 2019), 241.

2. For more on this, see the book on sanctification by Kent Eilers and Kyle Strobel forthcoming by Baker Academic in 2026.

3. Bavinck writes, "Viewed from the perspective of God's kingdom, natural morality has absolutely no value in God's eyes. . . . A wide chasm lies between the most highly developed moral life and the smallest seed of spiritual life. To obtain spiritual life, it is precisely the natural moral life that has to be entirely surrendered, put to death, and crucified with Christ. In that case, virtues are nothing but splendid vices." *Reformed Ethics*, 1:232.

4. *Luther's Works*, ed. and trans. Jaroslav Pelikan, vol. 26, *Lectures on Galatians: Chapters 1–4* (Saint Louis: Concordia Publishing House, 1963), 166.

5. Bruce Narramore addresses various aspects of the conscience, and though we do not follow him explicitly, he has helpful discussions of

Calvin's and Bonhoeffer's views of the conscience, as well as a helpful discussion of the relation of the conscience to the law. See Narramore, *No Condemnation*, 183–243.

6. William Bridge, *The Works of William Bridge*, vol. 1 (Banner of Truth Trust, 2022), 14.

7. William Bridge writes, "Luther calls this aspect of sin, a sacrilegious aspect and beholding of sin. As now (says he) if a man take out of an holy place some goods, and bring them into his own house; this is sacrilege. So for me to go and take my sins from Christ, and lay them in mine own bosom, this is sacrilege, says Luther." *Works of William Bridge*, 1:13.

8. *Dietrich Bonhoeffer Works*, ed. John W. de Gruchy, vol. 3, *Creation and Fall: A Theological Exposition of Genesis 1–3* (Fortress, 2004), 128.

9. *Dietrich Bonhoeffer Works*, 3:128.

10. Grant Macaskill, *Living in Union with Christ: Paul's Gospel and Christian Moral Identity* (Baker Academic, 2019), viii.

11. Macaskill, *Living in Union*, viii.

12. Macaskill, *Living in Union*, ix.

Chapter 7 Avoiding God in Our Devotion

1. William Perkins, "A Declaration of Certain Spiritual Desertions, Serving to Terrify All Drowsy Protestants, and to Comfort Them Which Mourn for Their Sins," in *Treatise Tending unto a Declaration . . .* (Printed by the Widdow Orwin for John Porter and John Legate, 1595), 178.

2. Perkins, "Certain Spiritual Desertions," 180–81.

3. Perkins, "Certain Spiritual Desertions," 176.

4. In path 1 at the end of this book, we reference some of the key literature on developmental maturation in the Christian faith. John of the Cross has been a major figure in this regard, but most assume that his is the only paradigm and that only Roman Catholics have addressed these issues. That is far from true, as we show there. Our own approach is one that is broadly accepted in the Protestant tradition, even though there is a good deal of variation. Protestants had a broad vision of developmental maturation in the Christian faith, like we are presenting here, and that differs from the more specific and detailed accounts sometimes found in the Roman Catholic tradition.

5. It is significant that when the Corinthian Christians couldn't find love in their hearts, Paul revealed to them they did, in fact, love him. Paul tells them that he wrote to them "in order that your earnestness for us might be revealed to you in the sight of God" (2 Cor. 7:12). Paul, ever the pastor, knew that the Corinthian church needed to find love in their hearts and that they needed to find it in the sight of God. There is much

here to ponder about how wise and pastorally sensitive Paul is, especially in such a tenuous relationship as he had with the Corinthians. Even in strife he took it upon himself to help them see their own love for him.

Chapter 8 Avoiding God by Fixing Ourselves

1. "J. I. Packer: John Owen Showed Me My Heart," Banner of Truth book excerpts, August 25, 2023, https://banneroftruth.org/uk/resources/book-excerpts/2023/j-i-packer-john-owen-showed-me-my-heart/?fbclid=IwAR3dP1b5cVnFBG868I6_FEbUloL_YZlEzUxK3iPJDlJ8alNJjl8FJJzlZGo.

2. "John Owen Showed Me."

3. John Owen writes, "A man may be sensible of a lust, set himself against the eruptions of it, take care that it shall not break forth as it has done, but in the meantime suffer the same corrupted habit to vent itself some other way. . . . Men in [old] age do not usually persist in the pursuit of youthful lusts, although they have never mortified any one of them. And the same is the case of bartering of lusts, and leaving to serve one that a man may serve another. He that changes pride for worldliness, sensuality for Pharisaism, vanity in himself to the others, let him not think that he has mortified the sin that he seems to have left. He has changed his master, but is a servant still." *Overcoming Sin and Temptation* (Crossway, 2006), 71.

Chapter 9 Transformed by Love

1. Dallas Willard, *The Great Omission: Reclaiming Jesus's Essential Teachings on Discipleship* (HarperOne, 2014), 34.

2. In the words of Willard, transformation is through *"union with* God, not apart from him—not independently, on our own." *Renovation of the Heart: Putting on the Character of Christ* (NavPress, 2002), 82.

3. Of course, we would add that this vision of spiritual formation is by Scripture alone, keeping in mind that this is not Scripture *only* but rests on Scripture as the Word of God given to us by our Lord. The historic Protestant vision of Scripture alone (sola scriptura) is a vision we follow in our understanding of evangelical spiritual formation that is Word-centered and Spirit-empowered for a whole-life spiritual formation into the likeness of Jesus.

4. Willard, *Renovation of the Heart*, 22.

5. Thanks to Jamin Goggin for pointing out that this was the emphasis of the Puritan interpretive tradition. It also seems that what Jesus is doing here is what Paul does in 2 Cor. 7:12, where he wants the Corinthian church to know their love for him *"in the sight of God."* There is a pastoral brilliance at work in these passages that we can easily miss if we don't attend to them deeply.

Chapter 10 Walking the Path Ahead

1. Perhaps more than anyone else, John Calvin wonderfully focuses on the fact that Christ is salvation. See *Calvin: Institutes of the Christian Religion*, ed. John T. McNeill, trans. Ford Lewis Battles (Westminster Press, 1960), III.xi.1. (725).

2. The image of God "zapping" us is borrowed from our friend Steve Porter.

3. William Gurnall, *The Christian in Complete Armour* (Banner of Truth, 2022), 15.

4. Isaac Ambrose, *Looking Unto Jesus: A View of the Everlasting Gospel; Or, The Soul's Eyeing of Jesus, as Carrying on the Great Work of Man's Salvation, from First to Last* (Sprinkle, 1986), 430.

5. Francis Rous, *The Mystical Marriage: Experimental Discoveries of the Heavenly Marriage Between a Soul and Her Savior* (William Jones, 1631), chap. 5, https://www.monergism.com/thethreshold/sdg/rous/The%20Mystical%20Marriage%20-%20Francis%20Rous.pdf.

6. Wilhelmus à Brakel, *The Christian's Reasonable Service*, trans. Bartel Elshout, vol. 4, *Ethics and Eschatology* (Reformation Heritage Books, 2015), 146.

7. Christian's Reasonable Service, 4:148.

8. Christian's Reasonable Service, 4:148.

9. Christian's Reasonable Service, 4:148.

10. Christian's Reasonable Service, 4:149, 151.

11. Christian's Reasonable Service, 4:151.

12. Christian's Reasonable Service, 4:160.

13. Christian's Reasonable Service, 4:161–62.

14. Christian's Reasonable Service, 4:163. When this happens, he explains, "It becomes more a natural work and approximates the virtuousness of unconverted people."

15. Christian's Reasonable Service, 4:171.

16. Christian's Reasonable Service, 4:174.

17. Christian's Reasonable Service, 4:268.

18. "Against the Antinomians," in *Martin Luther's Basic Theological Writings*, 3rd ed., ed. Timothy F. Lull and William R. Russell (Fortress, 2012), 178.

19. The Complete Works of Richard Sibbes, ed. Alexander Balloch Grosart, vol. 1 (James Nichol, 1862), 95.

20. Works of Richard Sibbes, 5:207.

21. *John Wesley's Sermons: An Anthology*, ed. Albert C. Outler and Richard P. Heitzenrater (Abingdon, 1991), 37.

22. *John Wesley's Sermons*, 37.

23. Charles Haddon Spurgeon, "The Desire of the Soul in Spiritual Darkness," June 24, 1855 sermon, The Spurgeon Center, accessed May 28, 2024, https://www.spurgeon.org/resource-library/sermons/the-desire -of-the-soul-in-spiritual-darkness/#flipbook/.

24. See Jonathan Edwards's sermon "Charity Contrary to an Envious Spirit" in *Charity and Its Fruits: Living in the Light of God's Love*, ed. Kyle Strobel (Crossway, 2012), 125–38.

KYLE STROBEL is the director of the Institute for Spiritual Formation and a professor of spiritual theology and formation at Talbot School of Theology at Biola University. A popular speaker, Strobel is the author of *Formed for the Glory of God* and coauthor of *Beloved Dust* and *The Way of the Dragon or the Way of the Lamb*. He has written for *Relevant*, Pastors.com, *Christianity Today*, The Gospel Coalition, DeeperStory.com, and others. He and his family live in Fullerton, California, where he serves on the preaching team of Redeemer Church. He is the coauthor with John Coe of *Where Prayer Becomes Real* and *When God Seems Distant*.

─── **Connect with Kyle:** ───

📖 KyleStrobel.substack.com

ⓕ @KyleCStrobel

📷 @KyleStrobel

✕ @KyleStrobel

JOHN COE is a professor of spiritual theology and philosophy at Talbot School of Theology and Rosemead School of Psychology at Biola University. A leading expert on spiritual formation, he is a popular speaker on the topic at churches, retreats, and seminaries across the nation. He holds three master's degrees (in Bible, theology, and philosophy) and a PhD in philosophy from the University of California, Irvine. He lives in La Mirada, California. He is the coauthor with Kyle Strobel of *Where Prayer Becomes Real* and *When God Seems Distant*.

For more information about the Institute for Spiritual Formation at Talbot School of Theology, visit biola.edu/talbot/academics/isf.